OUR
BETTER
ANGELS

OUR

BETTER

ANGELS

Seven Simple Virtues That Will
Change Your Life and the World

JONATHAN RECKFORD,
CEO of Habitat for Humanity

with a Foreword by
JIMMY CARTER

ST. MARTIN'S
ESSENTIALS
New York

This book is dedicated to the better angels within us all.

Contents

Foreword

Ordinary people can accomplish extraordinary things. Over the course of my life, I've witnessed just how true that is. These days, it seems to me that it's more important than ever that we remember it.

It's understandable that we sometimes feel helpless. Our world is full of issues that are not easy to solve. But it is also full of people like you and me who can make a start. Rosalynn and I have always believed in doing whatever we can for as long as we can to help those around us and to change this world for the better. One of the ways we've been able to do that most consistently has been through our involvement with Habitat for Humanity. This book is full of the kind of transformative stories that we've seen again and again in our more than thirty-five years of building with them around the world. I always feel, after a build, that I've received as much as I have given—or more. That's the feeling that keeps me coming back.

It's also the feeling that keeps me thinking about the kind of help that Habitat offers: one person offering their hand to another in a time of need and doing so in a way that has a positive effect on everyone fortunate enough to be a part of it. That's what this world needs more of.

The commentary below was inspired in the days immediately after Hurricane Harvey caused such extensive destruction in Houston and in so many other communities in its path. In the aftermath of that 2017 storm—and of so many others before and since—I find inspiration. The way we respond to a disaster should be a template for the way we respond to each other every day. It really could be that simple. And that profound.

There are always those in need of help. There are always those in a position to offer it.

When a disaster like Harvey strikes, I often see glimpses of the world I first knew.

One of the things I remember most clearly about my childhood in rural Georgia was the notion that neighbors were more than just the folks who lived next door or down the road. Neighbors were people you could count on—and people who could count on you—whenever a need arose.

It was hard to feel truly alone with your troubles in such a close-knit place. No one ever had very much, but everyone felt a kinship, a responsibility, to each other that I believe helped shape how I see the world today.

I think it's how most of us see the world in the days after something like Harvey. Who could possibly remain unmoved by the scenes of damage and despair that come out of the affected areas? And yet there are also equally powerful images of regular people—individuals just like you and me—who come alongside those who are suffering and offer comfort, support, and resources.

When the water rises, so do our better angels. I've seen it again and again. We all have. Pick a past disaster, and I'll tell you at least a dozen stories that stand as living testaments to our collective compassion, generosity—and unity.

And it's not just disasters. Rosalynn and I have seen this impulse in our work around the globe. Anytime people come together in common purpose, miracles happen. We've seen elections proceed fairly, houses go up, diseases nearly disappear. But only because people of goodwill make it so.

Unfortunately, we all know that's not the world we live in every day. Instead, we seem trapped in a never-ending storm of rancor, divisiveness, and distraction. How much could we accomplish together, though, if we were able to see the world every day the way we see the world after a disaster? Neighbors in need. People with resources. All of us in this together.

This is what the people of Texas and Louisiana deserve from us as they begin the long road of recovery.

They deserve our best selves, the ones who see suffering and move to address it, the ones who understand their responsibility to help the most vulnerable among us, to help their neighbors. These disasters don't disappear when the flood waters recede—and neither should our better angels.

The good that comes from those times of action creates a healing halo—for those who are suffering and for those who are able to help. In our work with The Carter Center and Habitat for Humanity, Rosalynn and I always get back so much more than we give. The joy of helping others is truly a privilege that we cherish, and we know just how much you, how much all of us, can benefit from that same feeling.

Habitat has always been the most effective way for me and Rosalynn to live out our faith. The response to Harvey is a perfect opportunity for you to join us. When you help Habitat help families struggling in the wake of this storm, you change the world.

Get busy helping someone else and see—over time—the things you might have in common, instead of only the things that might divide you. Remember what can happen when we love our neighbors as ourselves. There are storms that bring us together and storms that divide us. We have a chance now to choose. Harvey already has reminded us what we're capable of when we come together.

The recovery ahead will be long. Our neighbors need to know they can count on us. The families affected will need our help and our attention as the work of rebuilding unfolds. If we hold our focus on the important matters at hand, we can use the power of the people to create that world we all know exists—if we will simply give it life.

In my life, I have always worked toward that world, and Habitat has always been one of the best ways I know to put my beliefs and principles into practice. The seven virtues highlighted in this book—kindness, community, empowerment, joy, respect, generosity, and service—certainly live on their build sites, but they are also virtues that must live in each of us every day. They are the virtues that will light our path.

My hope is that as you read these stories, you will begin to see the opportunities that surround you. That you will be moved, as Rosalynn and I have been, to become a part of something that doesn't just celebrate these virtues but actively creates and encourages them. Take your time and talents out into the world. Join forces with individuals like the ones you will read about in these pages.

The truth is that we need not wait for a disaster to offer up ourselves as instruments of change, of everyday miracles in the everyday making. Another thing that Habitat always reminds me of is that there are those in your community, closer than you think, who only seek your openness, your companionship, and your willingness to get involved. If you offer your hand, they will offer theirs. Others will, too. And those are the connections that will heal us all.

—Jimmy Carter

Introduction

THE NEWS WE see and read—the tone of the public discourse—can be dispiriting. But in my day-to-day work at Habitat for Humanity I get to witness firsthand stories that defy the doom and gloom.

These stories nurture my spirit. They make me smile. They fill me with hope. They help me see how good the world can be and how much power we the people have to create the world we want and need.

In this book I share stories that show how it's possible to build friendship instead of creating division. How it's possible to communicate when you don't speak the same language. How it's possible to change a person's life without giving up your own, and how it's possible to change your own life. How it's possible to choose love over hate, to see the best in people instead of the worst, and to build houses, communities, and relationships from a place of common shared values.

When I was deciding what stories would best illustrate these possibilities for hope and love, I had to stop and think: What "shared values" really capture the ways we can find common ground?

They had to be simple. They had to be something each of us could actually "do." I finally identified seven simple virtues we can put into action. These virtues make the stories in this book possible, and they can create happier stories in our own lives. They are simple virtues—kindness, community, empowerment, joy, respect, generosity, and service—but they are powerful.

To start with the simplest, practicing *kindness* may be the easiest way to change your entire outlook on life—or somebody else's. Even the smallest act shows that you are acknowledging another person. That you care about them. Dorothy Howard, whom you'll meet on page 16, was stunned by the kindness of volunteers and Habitat staff. Before they helped her move into her new home, she says, she never knew there was such a thing as love from strangers. What's it like to grow up never knowing that anyone other than your family cares about you? What's it like for the rest of us to know what we could be doing to change that for the people who feel overlooked and unloved in the world? One act of kindness can change a person's life—even if only for a moment.

Community means a connection to the rest of the world. If we can nurture our connections and be a part of our community, if we can be neighbors to one another, we can make our surroundings better for all of us. When Angel Meza, page 52, felt like she and her kids were adrift and on their own, instead of turning inward they started volunteering—and ended up being embraced by the community they were serving.

I'm in a lucky position when it comes to witnessing the virtue of *empowerment*. The stories we hear of kids like Antonia Cuffee, page 85, who with only a little bit of help entirely change the trajectory of their whole family, make me ask myself: How many kids with so much potential are slipping through the cracks? And how can we catch them?

There's *joy* in almost every Habitat story in some form or another. And sometimes, as in the case of Donna Ricca, joy finds us in the most unlikely places, as long as we are open to embracing it. You'll meet Donna on page 114.

When I think of current events, I think about how the virtue of *respect* plays a role in healing what is hurting us. Respect establishes common ground in places as far away as India and Vietnam and as close as our own neighborhoods. The way a group of neighbors in Durham, North Carolina, built each other up after a devastating loss is just one example of how exposure to those who are different from ourselves helps us celebrate common ground. Their story is on page 156.

Generosity, to me, is more than giving something away. It's a state of spirit that we bring with us to every encounter. Whether it's a work relationship or a marriage or anywhere two or more people gather, if you start with an attitude of

"What am I getting out of this?" it's very tough to have a successful relationship. If your attitude is "What can I do for my partner?" it's much more likely to be successful. When we approach the world with an outward sense of giving rather than an inward sense of keeping our gifts to ourselves, we can face the toughest challenges from a place of peace—even if that means facing death, as it did for Bob Karlstrand. His story is on page 179.

Finally, *service* is the place where all these virtues can come to life. If you don't really feel the other virtues, if you're not able to conjure up the feelings of kindness, community, empowerment, joy, respect, or generosity on command, try doing just one thing for someone else. Even if your heart is not in it and it's a pragmatic exercise, perform an act of service and see if these other virtues show up. When Taylor Thompson's world was turned upside down, he felt anything but virtuous. As you'll see on page 207, he felt lost, angry, and confused. He felt helpless to change anything, but he had to do something, anything. And by doing something, he found more than he was looking for.

The people in these stories were searching for something, and through these virtues they found a sense of home within themselves. They were able to ground themselves in a place from which they could do good things big and small for their families and contribute to their communities and the world. I can relate because until I found my home in Habitat, I was also searching.

After college, I had planned to go to law school so I

could enter politics. I quickly realized I didn't want to be a lawyer, and even though I had never considered going into business, I unexpectedly talked my way into a job in finance. It was a great opportunity, but I was working an insane amount of hours and not leading the kind of life I'd imagined.

I applied for a scholarship to work abroad and was lucky enough to get it. The Henry Luce Foundation sponsors fifteen young American leaders annually to work in Asia to promote cross-cultural resources and understanding. I ended up in South Korea.

It was a time of significant growth and sometimes loneliness. It gave me the space and distance to reflect on my life. My friendship with another American there, a professor teaching at a Korean university, was a gift for me. We had a standing appointment every Monday night to get together and talk about theology and faith.

I came back to the States with the mindset that I needed to do something that mattered, and for that, I needed more skills. I went back to school, to one of the only business schools that believed we needed more professional management of nonprofits—not a mainstream view at the time. I began my career in business so I could gain the skills I'd need in my mission that mattered. I learned a huge amount helping start or grow new businesses for different companies.

After my last company was acquired I went on a short-term service trip to rural India. I came back knowing I wanted to do something related to alleviating poverty and making a difference for low-income families around the world.

The only problem was that no one wanted me to run their mission. So I took that time to be a stay-at-home dad. By this point, my wife, Ashley, and I had three small children. I loved the time I got to spend with them, but I soon learned just how challenging being a stay-at-home parent is. I also spent a lot of time volunteering at our very large local church. Unexpectedly, they asked if I'd be willing to be their executive pastor so the lead pastor could focus on being the spiritual leader without having to manage all the ministries. Most of the people I trusted for advice thought this was a bad career decision, but it seemed clear that the church was where I was called to serve at that time.

Two years later an executive recruiter called out of the blue. Did I know anyone who might be interested in leading Habitat for Humanity? I felt the adrenaline running down my back as she talked. "Does it have to be somebody famous?" I asked. To my surprise, she said no. I went home and wrote the recruiter a passionate two-page letter that basically said this was the kind of job God had been preparing me for my entire life. Then I prayed.

This is my fourteenth year at Habitat, and there is nothing that I'd rather be doing. I finally found my mission that mattered.

Habitat itself started from a mission. Clarence Jordan, a farmer and biblical scholar, founded Koinonia, an interracial Christian farming community, in 1942 near Americus, Georgia. It goes without saying, Jordan was a man radically ahead of his time. When Millard and Linda Fuller came to Koinonia in the sixties, they worked with Jordan to develop the idea of *partnership housing.* They realized that one of the best ways to help low-income people was to offer them a partnership, a hand up rather than a handout. Instead of building houses and giving them away, the organization would help low-income people finance a home with an affordable mortgage, and together they would build the home. This was the key idea behind the organization that would become Habitat for Humanity.

What quickly became clear as Habitat grew beyond Americus, as well as through an outpost in Zaire, Africa, was that these partnerships between the poor and those with greater means gave the poor more than affordable housing and gave the contributors more than something to do with their money. It generated countless acts of the seven virtues in this book between people who might never have come into contact with one another. Since its official founding in 1976, Habitat has helped more than 22 million people build or improve their homes.

President and Mrs. Carter have been deeply involved in Habitat for more than thirty-five years. President Carter has repeated over the years that for him, Habitat is the best way he knows to put his faith into action. And "action" is the appropriate word when it comes to our ninety-five-year-old thirty-ninth president of the United States.

There was a legendary Carter Work Project in Manila, Philippines. It was brutally hot and late in the day, and everyone was exhausted and getting on the buses to go back to their hotels. President Carter walked onto every single bus and asked everyone to please get off the bus and keep working so the project could stay on track for the week. He made his request politely but . . . firmly. For him, building isn't an abstract symbol of goodwill. It is a concrete action of service. If a Carter Work Project doesn't deliver on building the houses, then it's just a publicity stunt. President Carter is nothing if not humble. A publicity stunt is not something he's interested in, in any shape or form.

He gives a devotion the first morning of each work project, and it's always fantastic. There's no one who wouldn't be motivated to get to work after hearing his morning message. He's like a coach who believes you will win, so you better get out there and win because you wouldn't want to prove him wrong or disappoint him.

He realizes people are excited to be on the builds and to see him and Mrs. Carter, so he sets aside specific times for taking photos with each house team at the end of the week. Otherwise, he says, "If you're taking pictures you're not working." One of my craziest days with him was when we were doing a work project in a wide-ranging area we'd somewhat loosely defined as the Mekong River region. In a matter of twenty-four hours, we were in Thailand, Vietnam, and China. I was exhausted, but it's hard to complain when the eighty-five-year-old next to you is raring to go.

One of the sweetest moments from the Carter Work Projects I've witnessed, and I get to see it every single year, is at the end of the day when the work is wrapped up and President and Mrs. Carter walk away from the build site together, holding hands. They continue to be role models not only to Habitat as an organization but also to me and every other individual who gets to witness their love for each other, their faith in action, and their united desire to help people.

The values they represent and that I have selected for this book are universal. For President Carter and me, they are an extension of our Christian faith, but Habitat has always been what we call "radically inclusive," meaning we welcome volunteers, supporters, and the families we build with from all backgrounds, and from all faiths and none.

Almost every faith on this planet holds these seven virtues in high esteem in some form. For everyone, even those with no faith, these values celebrate our shared humanity. At their most pragmatic level, they help us create connections with one another that help us get along and coexist in a more pleasant and effective way.

The significance of what President Carter said in his foreword, "When the waters rise, so do our better angels," speaks to this idea of neighborly coexisting. In the face of a crisis, all the differences between us disappear and we come together to help one another. Or we're on the receiving end of that help.

When the water's coming up and your neighbor arrives

by boat to rescue you, you don't ask whether they are Christian or not, gay or straight, or who they voted for in the presidential election. You don't care what they look like or how much money they make. You jump in the boat and say thank you. You realize there are people who care about you for no other reason than that you are their fellow human being. You remember next time the water rises what your neighbor did for you, and you decide you'll do the same for someone else in need.

Sometimes it takes a crisis to get us to pay attention to our shared humanity. Crises can be great reminders of what we can accomplish when we work together.

The phrase "our better angels" comes from President Lincoln's first inaugural address. Our nation was on the verge of war. Several states had seceded. "We are not enemies," he said, "but friends. We must not be enemies. Though passion may have strained, it must not break our bonds of affection." Then he expressed the hope that we could all remember our shared unity if we would hearken to "the better angels of our nature."

It's my hope that if we can anchor ourselves in the shared values of these seven virtues, then moving forward, we can be led by our better angels instead of by our personal self-interest, disagreements, and disappointments. Elite athletes practice their skills, then practice them some more, until they are deeply embedded in their muscle memory. In that same way, I think if we practice these virtues, we can let go of our self-interested desires and instead become adept at finding common ground.

You can read this book straight through or start with whichever chapter speaks to you most. You can read it in any order and pick it up at any time. My purpose is not to preach or tell anyone how to be or act; it is simply to share what I've been privileged to learn through the example of the people in these stories. If you're like me, certain stories will really hit you, and you'll want to read them over and over again to remind you what's possible when we let our better angels be our guide.

I

Kindness

WHEN IT COMES to simple virtues, kindness may be the simplest of them all. What could be more basic than doing small acts for others without expecting anything in return? But can small acts really affect anything in the long run?

We don't know what ripple effects even a tiny kindness may produce for the person on the receiving end. If you stop and give someone change for a parking meter or help someone struggling with an armful of packages, maybe that kindness is forgotten the next minute. Or maybe not. What if the person was having a particularly frustrating day and your tiny gesture helped them feel better and move forward rather than give in to their exasperation and take it out on someone else?

And what about the ripple effects for the person doing a kindness?

Well, for starters, I truly believe practicing kindness can change our brains. When we are kind, it makes us happy.

It makes us think less about ourselves. We stop asking, "What's missing in my life?" and start asking, "What can I give?" We become thankful for all we have rather than bitter over what we don't have. It's hard to do bad things when we're feeling grateful. It's easy to do good things when we're feeling grateful.

When we step outside of our own selves and are kind to people who don't look like us or have the same religion, politics, socioeconomic status, or experiences we have, it breaks down the barriers between "us" and "them." In fact, most of the time when you're being kind, you're not thinking about any of those things anyway. That stuff doesn't matter. You're simply a person being kind to another person.

When we give of ourselves, our kindness can become a force for healing. It contributes to that halo of hope President Carter wrote about. Think about the mosques that raised money for the victims of the synagogue shooting in Pittsburgh. In only four days following the attack, Muslims raised over $200,000 for their Jewish brothers and sisters.

The Prophet Mohammed said to do good to "neighbors who are near" and "neighbors who are strangers." He also said that "he is not a believer who eats his fill while his neighbor is hungry."

The Dalai Lama says, "My religion is very simple. My religion is kindness."

In the Christian New Testament, Jesus says there are two great commandments that basically override everything else. The first is to love God with all of your heart, soul, and mind, and the close second is "You shall love your neighbor as yourself." No matter what your faith, your tradition, or your belief system, kindness is at the heart of our best selves in this world we live in.

The Jewish faith may put it best with the Hebrew word *mitzvah*. Most people use the word to mean "a good deed." Its literal translation is "commandment." According to many scholars, however, it comes from the root word *tzavata*, which means "connection."

When we commit an act of kindness, we may simply be doing a good deed. We may be following a commandment to love our neighbors as ourselves. But sometimes an act of kindness feels like much more than taking an action or obeying a rule. Maybe that's because it creates a connection. We connect to our fellow man, to the best part of ourselves, and to some greater universe beyond our understanding where light chases out the darkness.

With practice, kindness can become a part of who we are and what we do. Through even small acts of kindness we can add to the healing halo and create big changes in the world. In the following stories, acts of kindness make ripples whose ultimate effects on doers and receivers we may never know. Those ripples may still be lapping onto the shores of distant beaches, a never-ending series of gentle waves, washing up gifts of treasure.

Dorothy Howard thought she knew the meaning of "love thy neighbor," but it took a Christmas mystery for her to truly get to the heart of the matter.

Christmas with a Catch

Dorothy Howard's Houston neighborhood wasn't known for Christmas miracles, and yet Christmas Eve, there on the street in front of her apartment building was Tom from Habitat for Humanity. Behind his truck was an empty trailer, ready to transport her belongings. Dorothy wasn't sad for a minute to leave this old apartment to move to her new home, a home she'd helped build with her own two hands and that she'd saved precious funds to buy. Still, it felt like a step into the unknown. Add to that, Tom had called her a few days earlier to let her know her house would be ready ahead of schedule if she wanted to go ahead and move in. Now, here she was on the eve of her new life, but she knew from experience that most miracles had a catch.

She commandeered her eight grandchildren. Small ones carried boxes out to the trailer, and older ones helped Tom carry the few pieces of furniture they were taking. It didn't take long for them to empty out the small apartment. As Tom tied down all of their possessions on the trailer, Dorothy was struck by how much room was left.

She said a silent prayer of thanks as they piled into Tom's truck. At fifty years old, she was starting life from scratch again. She was raising eight grandchildren instead of her own children this time around. It did feel like a miracle that her Habitat home was ready early, that she and the children would get to wake up Christmas morning in a new house in a new neighborhood, that the children wouldn't have to remain inside on Christmas morning to stay safe from guns and drugs on the street.

Instead of thinking about how empty those new rooms would be with only her scant possessions, she thought about how spacious they would feel. She thought of how wonderful the first morning with the second bathroom would be after all the endless mornings of the children fussing at each other and elbowing their way in and out of the single bathroom in their apartment. Filling the new house with beds, a table where they could eat and the kids could do their homework—that could all come later. She would make sure it did. For now, she focused on the miracle at hand. A new neighborhood, a new start for her family.

On the way to the house, Tom broke her out of her thoughts. "There is one thing," he said.

Here it comes, she thought. Maybe her Christmas miracle had been too good to be true. She told herself that whatever this one thing was, it was not going to keep them from waking up in their new place Christmas morning. She wouldn't let a bump in the road keep them from moving on. She'd experienced plenty of those, and she knew how to get herself over them and keep on going.

"Since it's Christmas Eve, we couldn't get the gas

hooked up," he said. "So there's no heat—and the oven and the stove won't work for cooking. I'm sorry, Dorothy."

"Oh, don't you worry about that," she said. "We'll be fine." She'd been planning on doing a bunch of Christmas cooking to celebrate their new home. That would have to wait. So be it. And they'd been sleeping on top of each other in their crowded apartment for over a year—they could snuggle up a few more nights to stay warm. But she said another silent prayer, asking for no more surprises, please. Little did she know what was still to come.

Dorothy felt flush with pride as they pulled up to the new house. It was so perfect. So neat and bright. It was one story with two windows facing the street. It had a front yard and a backyard. Tom had barely stopped the truck before Dorothy opened the door to get out.

Bring on the weather, the cold food—there was nothing that could dampen the joy Dorothy felt arriving at her new home. Maybe Christmas miracles were real after all. Owning this beautiful home she had saved for and helped build, and getting to give her grandchildren a safe place to live and play—it felt like things couldn't get any better.

Then they did. There to greet her was a group of volunteers waiting to unload the trailer and carry boxes inside. Dorothy couldn't believe that these people would spend their Christmas Eve coming over here to help her, people she'd never met before. She smiled at them and nodded her head in thanks—right now she had to get inside her new house.

She walked through the open door, and the tears she'd always been able to hold back came rolling down her face. Actually, these were new tears. They were happy tears, and she let them come.

The kitchen was so big, with brand-new appliances and clean, pretty cabinets. She had never been the first one to use anything in a house. This kitchen would be hers to use, to keep, to care for, to fill with food and love and all the generations of her family.

She decided the first thing she would buy when she saved the money would be a dining room table. She could already imagine her grandchildren sitting around it, passing food and talking about their day at school. She could imagine them doing their homework there, studying hard while she worked in the kitchen, cooking up dishes that would fill the house with their sweet smell.

She peered into her new bedroom. There was a bed in it, a bed of her very own. She hurried to the other bedrooms like a child on Christmas morning. They had beds, too! Beautiful bunk beds that meant no one would have to share.

When had Tom and the volunteers managed to do this?

The surprises didn't end there. She gasped when she saw the washer and dryer. She had never owned a washer and dryer. A washer and dryer changed everything. It meant they wouldn't have to wear clothes over and over without being washed. It meant she wouldn't have to haul mountains of clothes to the laundromat. Wouldn't have to save quarters or sit in the hot laundromat for hours, claiming the machines that worked and waiting for her loads to finish.

This last bit of her Christmas miracle truly felt like more than she could ever have hoped for. As if Santa had guessed what that secret thing was that wasn't even on her list.

Outside the children were running around the yard in circles, just because they could.

Volunteers started moving things in, and Dorothy began organizing the boxes. She was putting them in the right rooms when all of a sudden here came Tom. He dumped an armful of two electric skillets and a Crock-Pot on the kitchen counter. Then he ran back to his truck and came back with another Crock-Pot, electric blankets, and a space heater.

"What's all this?" Dorothy asked.

"I just raided my wife's kitchen. This way you can cook a Christmas dinner. And stay warm."

"You what?" Dorothy eyed the skillets and Crock-Pots, dumbfounded at what she was seeing. There would be a Christmas feast after all.

Dorothy had always been a woman of faith who trusted in God, but even for her this felt entirely unfamiliar. She looked hard at Tom. She had never met people like him and the volunteers. She had never before witnessed the love people could have for total strangers.

In this house furnished by strangers, she would go on to host family get-togethers, neighborhood parties, reunions, and holiday feasts. Over the years, she would have forty-one great-grandchildren and forty-four great-great-grands. They would know the power of a love for others *just because* and know how it felt to receive it and how to give it. And they would be able to share that love with neighbors, with strangers, with the world.

So in the end, Dorothy's Christmas miracle did have a catch . . . it wasn't just for Christmas. It would live on and keep going, a Christmas gift that turned into a lifetime of miracles.

A few days after Dorothy and her family moved into the new house, when Dorothy was still enjoying the sensation of touching every bed and every now and then lifting the lid of her new washing machine as if to convince herself it hadn't all been a dream, there was a surprise delivery.

"What's this?" she asked as she opened the door to a waiting deliveryman.

It was a dinette set. A pair of newlyweds Dorothy didn't know had been at the dedication ceremony for her new house and felt like the place wasn't complete without a table for her family to gather around. They'd gone out and bought one for Dorothy. Kindness. Just because.

It breaks my heart a little bit when I think about how
amazed Dorothy was at the kindness of strangers.
If you don't think a few hours of volunteering for
someone makes a difference, or a few dollars put
in toward furniture or food or gifts for someone
who's trying to stay afloat, think of Dorothy. Think
how small acts can create a lifetime of miracles and
generations of people who truly understand what it
means to love thy neighbor.

Geta Heradea could be forgiven for
not being kind.

Winter in Mizies

She knew things couldn't get any worse. And yet time and
time again they had. Who was she fooling? Still, she'd told
her husband this was it, the last winter she could live like
this. The time for wishing and hoping was over.

Geta Heradea wasn't the only one in the northwest
Romanian village of Mizies in desperate need of change.
Despite its proximity to the pretty city of Beius and the
dramatic peaks of the Apuseni Mountains, Mizies in wintertime was anything but picturesque. Without running
water in their houses, villagers waited in line at the com-
munal water fountain to collect water and then carry it
home for drinking, bathing, and cooking. Drafty old

houses with rotting, leaky roofs and no reliable source of heat made people sick, tired, cold, and dejected. The simple tasks of life like washing clothes and getting them dry were exercises in maddening futility.

For Geta these tasks were even more challenging. She'd had enough.

The rays of sunshine in her gray world were her two boys. Geta was thankful they were healthy and attending school, Viorel in the village and his older brother, Cristian, in Beius. She was proud of them. But she couldn't help thinking how much more they might be able to learn if they had a warm place to study. If they could worry less about having enough to eat, would there be more room in their minds to dream bigger?

Making up her mind to do something—anything— was the easy part. She was a determined woman. She'd had to be since birth. But being determined to do something and making it happen were two very different things.

Bundled in a coat with a scarf over her head, she went to get the cart from behind their dilapidated two-room house. She leaned over to massage her left leg, urging it to warm up for the long walk to the village center to buy sawdust. One cartful would be enough for the next two days. She set off along the road. There was no way to avoid all of the potholes. She knew each one of them by heart. She dreaded this ritual of pulling the cart down the road, past other homes, limping on her lame leg. She didn't wave to her neighbors. She kept her head down, willing the lonely trek to be over and done with.

From her earliest memories, life had been a challenge. She'd been born paralyzed on the left side of her body, and she spent the first ten years of her life going through treatments and painful physical therapy to gain most of her movement back. Making it through those early years wasn't as difficult as the ones to follow. The school for children with disabilities was on the other side of the country from her parents. Over three hundred miles, nine hours, separated them.

Geta went on to get a job in a factory, but after only two years she'd become sick and had to stop working—her lame leg hadn't made the job any easier, either. Now her monthly pension of one million lei, about thirty US dollars, didn't go far for the family of four. Thank goodness for her husband, Ioan, and his job at a furniture factory.

Poor Ioan, Geta thought, almost to the village center now. His parents had separated when he was only two years old, and he and his brother had gone to live with his widowed grandfather in a one-room house. His grandfather did the best he could to raise the boys, but even as a young child Ioan had to work to earn money for the household. She and Ioan were hardly alone when it came to barely scratching together an existence in Romania.

Later in the week she would go to her neighbors' and tend their cows. Her leg would throb after the hours spent in the cold air, and they wouldn't have any money to pay her, as usual, but at least she could get a little extra food for their supper and some seed for her chickens. Geta was short on cash because she'd bought Cristian a new track suit, his first one ever, so he could start high school without being embarrassed about his clothes. That was money well spent.

Back home, Geta hauled the heavy sacks of sawdust one at a time into the house. The house had two rooms, but they could only afford to heat one, so they cooked, ate, did homework, and slept all in the same place. The bathroom was a shack in the backyard. She said a little prayer as she dumped sawdust into the barrel on three legs that served as their heater. A few years earlier they'd had a house fire that destroyed the roof. Ever since, whenever she left the house she worried about it catching fire again. Ioan had fixed the roof, but without money for new lumber he'd had to reuse the damaged wood.

She lit the sawdust in the barrel. She would go take her bath; maybe by the time she got back the room would be warm and her hair might dry. Her hopes and dreams for clawing her family out of their circumstances were kept alive by thoughts of her sweet boys.

She carried a bucket to the well Ioan had dug himself in the backyard. Chickens scratched the dirt around her as she collected water from the well. Thank goodness for the chickens and their eggs. They'd had a cow, purchased with painstakingly saved money, so they could have milk and the boys could grow healthy and strong. But the poor cow had gotten sick, stopped making milk, and finally died.

Now eggs were their source of protein; only at Christmas and Easter would they splurge and get a little meat.

She shuffled past the chickens and into the crumbling outbuilding that served as the bathroom. At least it gave her some privacy for bathing, if not warmth. She dumped the bucket of cold water into the washtub and stripped off her layers of clothes. Shivering as her bare skin made contact with the cold air, she let herself daydream of a bathroom with a flush toilet and a bathtub. What would it be like not to have to dodge the chickens and the dog to go to the bathroom? She used a cup to pour the frigid water over her head.

Back in the kitchen, Geta started their simple supper. It was early, but this way, the boys would have room at the table to do their homework instead of having to share space with her while she cooked. As she worked, she marveled at what a person could get used to. Gray skies, leaky roof, bathing in a washtub, living in only one room. Sadder yet, she thought, she had gotten used to living in anger. She tried to remember her younger self when despite her challenges she didn't worry so much. She was out of practice when it came to hope for the future. And if she wanted a chance for her sons to attend university, to have a better life than the one she and Ioan were living, she was running out of time to make it happen.

Since the boys needed to get their sleep for school, they all went to bed early. The boys slept in one bed and she and Ioan in the other. She and Ioan were tired anyway, so she rarely had trouble falling asleep. She cuddled against Ioan to get warm. She would need her rest. Walking was not easy for her, but neither was living like this.

She had decided. Tomorrow she would walk the two and a half miles to Beius and back. She'd heard about a Habitat for Humanity office there that helped people fix their homes or build new ones. If they could help people in the city, couldn't they help people out in the villages? She decided she had nothing to lose by finding out. She would walk as far as it took. She was not going to accept this way of life for her boys. She would find a way, a place for them to dream, to thrive, to live in sunshine instead of the dark cold.

Many months later it seemed everything had changed— and not just for Geta.

It turned out Habitat could help her. Volunteers from the organization had descended on the village, and Geta, Ioan, Cristian, and Viorel joined them in the hard work of building a new home. Every day and night in their old home was more bearable as they watched the daily progress on their new house. Seeing, touching, hammering on her new home made Geta feel like rays of sunshine were coursing through her battered body and setting her mind at peace. Curious neighbors watched as the walls went up. Little did they know, Geta had plans for them, too.

Immediately after moving into her family's new home, only days removed from her last solitary sawdust trip, Geta invited the village children into the house so they could do their homework in a warm place. She babysat younger children so their mothers could work outside the house and earn money. She invited neighbors to come use her running water and her miraculous brand-new washing machine. No one would have blamed her for holding her new possessions tightly within her new insulated home. But instead, she opened her doors wide open and shared all of it.

And she and Ioan didn't stop there. As they were able to let the sun shine through their new windows, their anger at life began to melt away, leaving in its place new room for caring not just for their family but the families around them. If her sons could have a place to thrive and dream, why shouldn't her neighbors' sons and daughters have the same?

She and Ioan decided to donate the land around their home so Habitat could build more houses for the village. Neighbors Geta had previously avoided in her own despair now joined her on the worksites. The sweat equity Geta had poured into her own new home she now put into the new Habitat homes of her neighbors. Going to bed with her leg sore from hard work had never felt so good.

Volunteers came from the United States, Ireland, and other parts of Romania to help, and Geta's neighbors joined her in her new kitchen to make *kozunak,* a traditional Romanian sweet bread, to share with the volunteers.

After years of limping along that lonely potholed path, Geta was now forging a new path for the whole village.

Instead of being a subject of the community's pity, she was their leader. By the time she was finished hammering, cooking, and lobbying, Habitat had helped the village build homes for twenty-five families.

The Women's World Summit Foundation recognized Geta's efforts by awarding her its Prize for Women's Creativity in Rural Life for "building hope with hands and hammer," but for Geta the real prize was that hope itself.

No one was giving out hope in Mizies. Geta had to claim it for herself and her family, no matter how far she had to walk to get it. For those around her who also had forgotten what hope was, Geta was kind enough to share its spark with them and in the end warm the whole village. Winters in Mizies will never be the same.

Geta was barely out of the cold herself before she began sharing with her neighbors. Her kindness was exceedingly tangible—from giving the neighborhood children a warm place to study to working to make sure her neighbors had decent homes—but what about the intangibles? What about the way she inspired a whole village and showed them what was possible? It scares me to think: What would Mizies be like today if Geta hadn't taken that long, painful walk to Habitat? Or if she'd closed the doors to her new insulated home and kept in all the heat for herself? Kindness worked its magic through Geta and brought a whole village into the light.

———

Sometimes when the waters are rising, we don't realize we're going to need a lifeboat . . . or a school bus.

Angels on a Bus

She'd been able to hold it together. Until now.

Opening the old fishing shed, she broke down at the sight of the tangled pieces of nets, tackle boxes, fishing rods, and buckets jumbled together in a wet, stinking pile. The dark stain of the water line on the walls of the shed was above her head, maybe seven feet high. She imagined the bobbers, lures, and rods floating inside the old shed, swishing around in the roiling ocean water. Theirs had been the only shed on the street that hadn't washed away, simply because it was so heavy with fishing gear, lovingly accrued over the last fifty years. Fishing was pretty much the only thing her father, a Marine Corps veteran disabled from a stroke, could do for fun from his wheelchair. Now she wondered if he would ever get back here, ever be able to fish again.

Cleaning out the shed was the first time after Superstorm Sandy that Denise Gavala cried. She was more analytical than emotional, and that had helped her push through to this point. She had the personality to look at a challenge and figure it out. She'd been able to process and keep her goal in mind—to get her parents back in the house they'd built fifty years before in Ortley Beach, New Jersey. She wanted it to be exactly the way they'd left it before the storm.

Living and working an hour away, Denise had spent every weekend for the last four months after the storm at the house, accomplishing one task at a time. She hauled out all the ruined furniture, pulled up the carpet and dragged it to a massive debris pile on the sand-covered street, removed water-stained drywall and soaked insulation. She'd made a lot of progress, but now the remaining challenges of getting her parents back in their house loomed like another round of black storm clouds.

She was a positive person, but she knew she couldn't redo the kitchen herself or make the bathroom work again. She couldn't even get her father inside the house. What used to be a wheelchair ramp was gone. What used to be a yard was gone. All that surrounded the house was dead plants and sand. Lots of sand. Wheelchairs and sand—not a good combination. Still, having helped care for her dad the last nineteen years, getting his wheelchair in and out of cars and buildings, she knew there was nothing they couldn't overcome. She just wasn't sure how.

Then she got a phone call. Could she be at the house at 7:30 a.m. Wednesday? Some college kids on spring break from St. Bonaventure University wanted to build a wheelchair ramp for the house. She was intrigued by the offer but not all that hopeful. And the sight of them early that morning didn't help.

It was dark and cold when the beat-up bus pulled up. It was patched and painted different colors; Denise thought maybe it was the Partridge Family bus salvaged from the junkyard. About a dozen sleepy-eyed college kids piled out followed by their leader, Jim. They were so quiet. Denise hadn't had any volunteers help her before, and she wasn't sure what to do or say. The kids didn't seem to know what they were doing either, so they all stared at each other until Jim got the kids to start unloading the bus. They formed an assembly line, and out from the bus came bags of cement, sawhorses, shovels, buckets, and tools. Then they pulled out a circular saw.

"Whoa!" Denise said. "We don't have any electricity." She'd been right not to get her hopes up. The ramp would have to wait. She felt bad for the kids. What a waste of time.

Jim ignored her, though, and disappeared into the bus.

"We brought a generator," he said.

"Oh. Well. Where are you going to put this ramp?"

She and Jim had different opinions. Strong opinions. As they argued on the patch of sand that used to be the yard, the kids stood back, unnerved by the heated discussion and looking like they really wanted to get back on the bus. A cold spitting rain started up.

Finally, Denise and Jim came to an agreement. Denise wished she could just build the darn ramp herself.

Jim gave the kids very specific instructions. Only two or three of them had done construction work before, but Jim didn't seem to care. He gave them each a task. Cut this wood into twelve-inch pieces like this. Dig a hole here.

Denise wanted to help, so she asked Jim for a job. Watching somebody else work on her house was not something she was cool with. But they wouldn't let her help. They told her to rest, to let them do it. Grateful but frustrated, she went inside the unheated house and watched from the window.

Soon her aggravation eased into a curious appreciation. She marveled at Jim's way with the kids, most of whom had barely used a hammer before. He was patient with them, but also direct. He gave clear directions, and the kids were eager to follow them and do a good job.

The weather didn't improve as the morning wore on. The kids were getting covered with the wet sand. Having worked on the house so many weekends herself, Denise knew all too well the wretched feeling of cold, wet blue jeans. Still, the kids pressed forward with no complaints, only determined faces and moving bodies.

There wasn't a working bathroom anywhere in the neighborhood, just some porta-potties on the street. Denise offered to ferry the kids back and forth to the closest gas station so they could use a real bathroom and wash their hands with warm water. The kids didn't say much on the trips back and forth, but they appreciated the time in the warm car.

Unable to sit back and watch, Denise went to a deli that had recently reopened and bought hot sandwiches. The kids ate on the floor inside the house, cold but out of the rain. They were as quiet as they had been when they first arrived, and Denise didn't know how to break the silence. This being her first experience with volunteers, she still wasn't sure what her role was. They did seem to like the sandwiches, though.

Jim and the kids worked into the night. Denise resisted the urge to walk outside too often to check on their progress. Finally, in the dark, they finished the ramp. Denise was amazed at what this ragtag crew had accomplished in a single day, albeit a very long one.

The ramp was beautiful. It was better than the ramp that had been there before. The pilings were dug deep into the ground and set with concrete. If another hurricane came, this ramp was going nowhere.

She didn't have the words to express her mixture of awe, appreciation, and admiration, so she simply said to the group, ready to get back on the bus and find a warm place to sleep, "Thank you. Thank you so much."

"No, thank *you*," they all said.

They wiped off their equipment the best they could and dumped it in the bus and climbed in after it. There were more ramps to build.

These quiet kids who had no business building anything and yet had built a way for her father to get into his home of fifty years had kept thanking Denise instead of accepting her thanks. This baffled her. It felt like a riddle she needed to figure out.

The kids on the bus were the start of something. Soon after their work at the house, more bands of patchwork angels began coming through to help. The word had gotten out, and "Denise's house" became a destination for volunteers. "We heard you were fixing your parents' house so they could come back home, so here we are!"

After so many months in the cold and wet, working alone to complete huge tasks one small step at a time, Denise was stunned by this sudden influx of people who wanted so badly to help.

She'd always been a charitable person. It wasn't as if she didn't understand the desire to help those in need. But being on the receiving end of this much kindness and sacrifice was a new experience for her, and at first she was at a complete loss as to how to react. It felt strange to accept their help. Still, they wanted to help so intensely, she felt bad if she didn't accept the assistance they were offering.

The angels simply would not be deterred. They kept coming. *What can we do? What do you need?* Denise thought back to how Jim had been so direct and how the kids responded to his straightforward guidance. So when others came looking for things to do to help, she tried to emulate Jim, coming up with specific jobs. A retired US Marine and his wife and son drove up in their pickup one day wanting to help. Denise needed to dig some holes for pilings. They dug holes. A group from California spackled and sanded the walls. Volunteers from Samaritan's Purse, the Pay It Forward Foundation, and the veterans program from Habitat worked on the bathrooms and kitchen. Church groups, high school students, even grammar school kids showed up and did whatever needed doing.

A group of kids walking down the street wanted to help on a day Denise was trying to pull up the dead shrubs. The bushes had been firmly rooted in the yard for almost fifty years, and each one was a beast to pull out of the mounds of wet sand. The kids skedaddled. Denise didn't blame them.

But then they were back. With adults and machinery. In a matter of hours they removed every single one of the dry, craggy reminders of the storm's lethal touch. It would have taken Denise weeks to pull them all out herself.

A family came by to help, but the youngest little girl felt left out as her parents and older siblings worked. "Do you think you could help me wash the windows?" Denise asked. The little girl's face lit up. Even such a tiny child understood the gift of being kind. She understood the feeling of love that came from helping someone, from contributing, doing one little task that would help Denise's mama and daddy get home.

Denise started keeping count. So far, more than a hundred hands had worked on her parents' house, and it had all started with the kids on the bus. She wished she'd known then what she knew now about working with volunteers. She wished she could thank them for more than just giving up their spring break for cold, wet days building wheelchair ramps instead of partying on a sunny beach somewhere.

They'd given her a crash course in the care and feeding of angels that she'd had no idea she would need. They'd taught her that angels wanted to be helpful, wanted a job. So she started keeping a posterboard in the house with a list of tasks that needed to be done. She remembered that even though she and the kids from the bus had exchanged few words, the hot sandwiches they ate on the cold floor of the house had been a communication of sorts. It was one small way Denise could show her appreciation for their kindness without them telling her to sit down and relax. If they wouldn't let her work, then she would at least make sure they had a little warm food in their bellies.

So she set up a grill in the yard and grilled hot dogs for the volunteers. Once she had power, she set up Crock-Pots. After a crew of high school students annihilated a pot of chili in about five minutes, she made a mental note: the younger the volunteers, the more food to make.

It wasn't just the sandwiches Denise recalled when she remembered sharing lunch with the kids on the bus. She thought about the missed opportunity. What would she do differently if she could have that awkward lunch with them all over again?

Over lunches, she began asking the volunteers questions about themselves, where they came from, what jobs they did back home or what they were studying in school. She put a 10" × 14" picture of her parents on the wall inside the front door so the volunteers could see the people they were so selflessly helping get back home.

Denise was not a natural hugger. But she became one.

Before the kids had shown up, Denise had been a one-woman force, plodding along on her own, determined to get her parents home no matter how long it took. She hadn't wanted help.

How far would she have gotten on her own? Certainly not far enough to have any physical or emotional energy left over to help anyone else. That would have had to come much later. But now, with the hard work of all the angels, she was no longer a one-woman show. She could join the band of angels herself and pass along the kindness that had been shown to her.

Thanks to the efforts of many volunteers, the bathroom worked, the gas was hooked up, and the electricity was back on. She began inviting her neighbors whose houses still needed work to come over whenever they needed a place to get warm, have a rest, or get a hug.

She was also able to help people with the logistics of rebuilding their homes—what you had to do to get water back, who could help you with plumbing or Sheetrock. She even used her new network of angels to connect people in need with the right volunteer organizations.

Mostly, though, she gave people hope. They could sit in her warm living room and see what was possible. Denise would tell them that over a hundred hands had helped bring her home back to life, the hands and hearts of angels—that she hadn't done this alone, and they wouldn't have to do it alone either.

One question still lingered. Why did all the volunteers thank her when it should have been the other way around? This question only got more vexing as volunteers began leaving gifts. Denise should be the one giving *them* presents.

They left pictures, drawings, and psalms written inside the walls before they covered them in Sheetrock. One group baked her a cake. One day she went into the house to find plastic dinosaurs on all the windowsills. She called the two guys from Virginia who had been working on the house. "You know anything about these dinosaurs?" she asked.

They told her they always left a gift behind after volunteering, but the only store that was open was a dollar store, so plastic dinosaurs it was.

A month or so after her parents finally moved back in, they opened a cabinet and found a package. There was no note. Who had left it behind? How long had it been in the cabinet waiting for them to find it? Inside was a beautiful blue wheelchair lap blanket.

Even today, a few years after her father's passing, that blanket rests on his chair in the house, and his fishing equipment waits patiently in the rebuilt fishing shed, reminders that her parents did make it home and her father did fish again. But the house isn't just like it was before the storm: it's better than it was.

Before her parents moved back in, Denise was on the phone with her mother one day, giving her an update on everything. "Denise, I think you're having too much fun with this!" her mother said. She was right. There was something about caring for the people who were being so kind to her family and being able to help her neighbors in turn that beat back the destruction of the storm and instead opened up a new way forward.

The angels had given Denise the gift of learning to accept kindness and thereby be better able to give kindness. It felt good to feed the volunteers. It felt good to hug her neighbors and show them that there was hope and a hundred hands to help them get there. And it had all started with the angels on the bus.

The St. Bonaventure kids continue as a rotating crew of angels under Jim's guidance. Denise never forgot the lessons they taught her through their selfless spirit on that cold, wet day. The group follows natural disasters like storm chasers in their beat-up old bus to build ramps for those who can't quite get back home on their own. To this day, when Denise turns on the news and sees a flood, hurricane, or tornado affecting a community, she sends a little food-and-gas money to Jim's band of angels, because she knows that where there are people needing to get back home, that's where angels will be building a way.

2

Community

IN HIS FOREWORD, President Carter wrote about one of his
most vivid memories from his childhood: how difficult it
was to feel alone with your troubles when you were part of
a tight-knit neighborhood where everybody was someone
you could count on. When Mister Rogers created the show
that was all about making children feel safe and loved, he
didn't call it Mister Rogers's "House" or Mister Rogers's
"World"—it was *Mister Rogers' Neighborhood*. If it's been a
while since you've sung the words to the show's theme song,
they may be worth revisiting. They enjoin us to appreciate that we're here together anyway, so why shouldn't we
reach out to one another in love and friendship? Why not
be neighbors instead of people merely sharing space? What
is beautiful feels only more so when we share it.

But what does "neighbor" even mean in these crazy
days? What exactly is a neighborhood? How do you define
"community"? Does an online community count? Being

in a neighborhood, being part of the community, used to be a pretty simple fact of life. Without video games or air conditioning, kids played outside together. Parents sat on porches and waved at passersby. Families belonged to faith organizations and worshipped together. Adults belonged to civic groups. That's not to say life was better back then—there was discrimination in many social organizations, women had fewer opportunities for working, and bucking convention was not always well received, to say the least—but the fact remains that there was a level of community participation where almost anybody with any interest could be a part of something.

Being a part of the community, being a neighbor, was a two-way street. On the receiving end, you got the benefit of a sense of belonging and knowing that if trouble came your way, you had a whole community of neighbors to help you through it. On the giving end, you got to give back to your community in a very real way by taking care of it and making it a safe and loving place for you and your neighbors.

It's so easy to hang our heads and say, "But it's not like that anymore," and then reminisce about the good ol' days, lamenting the current state of things. The fact is, there are people out there, in neighborhoods across the globe, actively living out what it means to be part of the community. At Habitat, if we didn't believe in community, we'd have hung up our tool belts a long time ago. What drives us is not how many houses we have built but the people in houses, huts, and lousy apartments all over the world who have reclaimed the concept of community and shown the rest of us what it really means to be a neighbor. People like the ones in these stories—individuals who instead of moving away or hiding, raised their hands and stomped their feet and said, "This is unacceptable. Let's do something."

Habitat's spiritual founder, Clarence Jordan, wrote about what he called "divine irritation," a point where you get upset because things are bad—so bad, in fact, that you realize you'd better do something before it's too late. In a neighborhood it might be trash along the main thoroughfare. You called city hall, but nothing happened, and every time you drive by it makes you madder and madder until one day, you stop your car and start picking up the trash yourself. Somebody sees you, and the next week that person tackles another road. Before you know it, people are asking themselves why they didn't think to do the same thing, and they follow your lead and start doing it.

When we let those divine irritations ignite into a spark and step out of our own cars and our own houses, we can start a movement. Thank goodness for those divine irritations that bring neighbors together and then lift the whole community.

One of my favorite things that happens in a neighborhood where Habitat has been building new homes is that residents who were already there start fixing up their houses and yards. When the neighbors start painting their front doors and cutting their grass where before they'd let it go, it's like watching a tree you thought had died over the winter come back to life in the spring. It's a sure sign of that subtle change in mindset where the community believes things really could change for the better, and instead of passively accepting the status quo, they're coming out into their yards and streets to become part of that change.

We talk a lot about "critical mass" at Habitat, that tipping point where something good catches on and then takes on a life of its own. In Winston-Salem, North Carolina, for example, Habitat took part in a coalition with private developers to revitalize a neglected neighborhood. Habitat agreed to build sixteen homes, and in return, one of the developers committed to buying up surrounding homes and refurbishing them, and another developer agreed to build affordable rentals. Any one of those things wouldn't have made much of a splash, but together they could make an impression.

For young families to buy in and want to bring life back to the neighborhood, however, housing couldn't be the only factor. So the city hired more police officers to patrol the neighborhood. The school district hired a new principal to improve the neighborhood elementary school. In three years, the crime rate went down 70 percent. Habitat built fifty more houses and moved its local office to the neighborhood, where they could offer family services not only to Habitat families but to all the local residents. Having come together in a joint effort of people who cared about this community and wanted to be an integral part of its change, the neighborhood can now sustain itself and look to an even brighter future.

Newburgh, New York, is another example of a community taking charge of its own change. Formerly a bustling city on the cutting edge of industry, Newburgh had fallen on hard times. Architectural gems from its heyday had degenerated into uninhabitable structures blighted by graffiti, litter, and squatters. Newburgh natives Bill Murphy and Al Favata and longtime resident David Wager refused to let their community and its neglected historical structures crumble away. They established the Habitat affiliate in Newburgh and immediately set about restoring neighborhoods one house, one family at a time. When fellow native Deirdre Glenn heard people laughing and building on her block instead of fighting in the street, she couldn't help but join in and became the affiliate's first executive director. Newburgh native Corey Allen, neighborhood revitalization coordinator at the affiliate, helped bring back the sense of neighbors taking care of each other that he enjoyed as a child by organizing a self-sustaining neighborhood association of Habitat families and longtime residents working together. The association now operates on its own to advocate and manage improvement projects. One person standing up to do something can lead a whole block and then a whole community to a sense of pride and ownership.

It's not easy being a neighbor when you live in a neighborhood that's plagued by poverty and crime. When you're in survival mode, all you think about is keeping your family safe and fed. You keep your head down and mind your own business. Families who get to make the move to a neighborhood that is safe, whether that's through Habitat or some other means, understand the power of community better than anyone else. They appreciate that support system they've never had before.

Many Habitat families tell me how much they love their neighbors because they've been through the same struggles. They know how hard each one of them fought to get to this point in their lives. When they help take care of each other's yards and children and pets, it's not just a matter of "Well, that's what neighbors do." For them, it is a blessing they will never take for granted. These families who are all new to being neighbors can teach us a lot. Maybe we shouldn't take our neighborhoods and our community so lightly.

I believe it's time for us to restore what it means to be a neighbor today. And the people in these stories can inspire us. Do we stay inside our homes to fend for ourselves and not really care what's going on outside our walls? Or do we walk outside, look around, and see how we can help make our neighborhood a better place? Do we walk past our neighbors, looking down or at our phones, or do we look them in the eye and say, "Won't you be my neighbor?"

All of us are in this world, this community of ours, together. We don't have to go it alone. When we reach out and become neighbors, when we help one another, we create a better place that supports all of us and lifts us up when we need it most.

What happens when neighbors aren't just "like" family, they become family?

Granny and the Kingdom in the Sky

It's called the Kingdom in the Sky. In its hills lie diamonds. Peaches grow in the countryside. Crystal-clear water cascades down snow-capped mountains into streams teeming with trout. Round thatched-roof stone dwellings called rondavels dot the landscape. Sheep bells ring from the ridges above, as herd boys on horses tend their flocks. Aloe plants nestle among boulders like pinwheels. The Basotho people wear colorful wool blankets, a tradition started by King Moshoeshoe in the nineteenth century, and *mokorotlo,* conical woven straw hats whose shape reflects the surrounding mountains. Lesotho, a small country bordered on all sides by South Africa, could truly be a storybook kingdom.

Granny rises at five in the morning, a full, busy day ahead. The children rub their eyes and wake to the sound of Granny singing as she grinds the kernels of maize from her garden against the grindstone. She boils water in the pot over the fire, then pours in the meal to make their daily breakfast of *papa*. She makes sure the five oldest children get dressed for school in their uniforms and then shoos them out of the house so they're not late. She thinks of taking a quick break, but Kananelo and Nthebiseng, the two girls too young for school, call for her attention, and she is happy to give it.

The seven children range in age from two to fourteen, four boys and three girls. They are Granny's children, but they didn't start out that way.

These are dark days in the kingdom. In a nation of 2 million people, officials estimate there are 200,000 orphaned children, over 25 percent of children under the age of eighteen.

The life expectancy in Lesotho is one of the lowest in the world at 53.7 years. In this place so rich in culture, more than half of the people live below the poverty line. Three-quarters of the people live in rural areas, beautiful places fraught with perpetual challenges.

Women must often walk great distances to those bountiful streams to fetch water for drinking, cooking, and bathing. By the time the streams make their way to the capital city of Maseru, denim factories, a sheepskin tannery, a slaughterhouse, mines, mills, and runoff from sewage, dumpsites, and agriculture have diminished the quality of the water that began its trek as cold, clear snow melt from the majestic mountains. There is a large system of dams in the kingdom, but the water levels are still recovering from a drought, and much of that water is sold to South Africa. Access to drinking water and a sanitary latrine is not a given, especially in the countryside.

The herd boys make for a proud and pastoral image with their wool caps, blankets, rubber boots, and sure-footed horses, but that image belies the fact that many of them are sent to tend the family flock as early as the age of ten. Up in the hills, they can lead an isolated existence, missing out on friendships, family, and education.

Women do not have the same land ownership or inheritance rights as men. Nor do they typically share equity in marriage, so if a woman's husband dies, she and her children are often left homeless and without any recourse.

Granny's children are orphans. They are victims of the problems and the ripple effect of their symptoms that plague Lesotho—abuse, abandonment, poverty, and parental physical and mental illness. And perhaps the darkest cloud of all over this Kingdom in the Sky is HIV/AIDS. A devastating 25 percent of adults in Lesotho have HIV/AIDS, and 53 percent of children here have lost at least one parent to the disease.

After school, Granny's boys tend to her garden of spinach, carrots, beetroot, beans, and maize while Tsotliso, the eldest girl, looks after the younger ones as they color and sing quietly on the stoop. Granny finally takes a break from her cooking and cleaning and sits in a plastic chair in a slip of shade in the yard. She watches her children and smiles, proud and filled with love like a doting grandmother, but worried and filled with determination like a mother.

The fabric of this small country is stretched and fraying. The typical community of parents, children, grandparents, extended families, friends, and neighbors is falling apart. What happens to a family when parents die or get sick or go away? What happens when there is no granny, no auntie to take in the children? What do you do when HIV and AIDS pluck from the community people at its very core—the doctors, teachers, shopkeepers, bus drivers, and policemen? How does a community live when all of its grown-ups are dying or fading away? When there is no one to deliver a baby, fix a child breakfast, wipe away a tear? In this kingdom of rich traditions and proud people, how can communities continue when the traditional community support systems can no longer function?

As Granny fixes a supper of *papa* with spinach and beans mixed in, she watches her children bent over their homework. Tsotliso wants to be a nurse when she grows up. The oldest boy, Tsoanelo, wants to be a policeman. Tsepo and Moshoeshoe dream of being soldiers, and little Lehlohonolo thinks he might be a pastor. They are getting good grades in school. That is Granny's goal—for them to get a good education so they can have a good future. She says a prayer as she rocks side to side, stirring the steaming pot. *Keep them healthy, God, keep them learning, God, help them know you.*

Granny adopts the neighborhood children as her own not because there is no hope in this kingdom but because there is hope. These babies who could have gotten lost in the dark have a chance at a storybook ending for themselves and for the Kingdom in the Sky. At Granny's modest home, built by Habitat in a partnership with other nonprofits focused on supporting vulnerable children, she's raising the next generation of a community—a nurse to heal and care for the people, a policeman to protect the people, soldiers to keep the peace for the people, a pastor to tend to the people.

Maybe some traditions are ready to go by the wayside. The traditional community support systems may have been breaking in Lesotho, but heroes like Granny are creating new communities. Communities of love for one another and love for this enchanting kingdom in peril.

Granny is peopling the next page of Lesotho's story with vibrant, loving children who will grow to become the next chapter. Even if no one else can see a happy ending, Granny must, because she hasn't finished with her mission to rebuild her community.

Her next-door neighbor is currently caring for a one-year-old little girl whose mother suffers from illness and epilepsy and whose father abandoned her. When she turns two, this little one will become the ninth member of Granny's household. Her name is Rethabile, and in the Basotho language, *rethabile* means "we are happy."

When we started thinking about all the people who would populate this book with their stories, giving examples of how old-fashioned virtues in their lives changed things for the better, Angel Meza inevitably kept coming up. And not just because her name is Angel.

Angel is a natural-born neighbor. She cares about helping those around her. She wanted her children to develop talents they could share and be positive people who saw the best in others. She loves getting to know people from different backgrounds and feeling the sense of friendship and shared purpose that united them. Angel is the perfect neighbor. The only problem was that the perfect neighbor had no neighborhood of her own.

A Couch to Call Home

It wasn't easy to fall asleep on the floor, no matter how tired she was. Angel Meza of Denver, Colorado, thought she'd be used to it by now, but still she turned her body every few minutes, trying to get comfortable. For the kids, she was able to fake the feeling that sleeping in someone else's living room was a fun adventure. She read them a book and then tucked them in on the couch like little puppies snuggled together, overlapping legs and heads. But in the dark, as she tried to push the thoughts away from her mind, there was no faking the smell of the carpet, the ticking of the clock on the mantle, or the hulking shadow in the corner of the room that was their pile of belongings—all reminders that this was not her home. She kept their corner of stuff as neat and organized as possible. She made sure to get the kids up at dawn so by the time her friends woke up she had folded all the blankets and pillows, like they hadn't really been there, like they'd just popped by to say good morning. She'd almost forgotten what it felt like to fall asleep in your own bed. A bed.

She was grateful for the friends who took them in— God, was she grateful. And her kids were beautiful, smart, and healthy. She had so much to be thankful for, especially considering what they'd already been through. But she was determined that one day she would have her own couch, a new one, a big one. And it wouldn't be for sleeping. It would be for sitting, for kicking their feet up, for watching movies together, for having the kids' friends over, for sinking into the cushions and closing her eyes and breathing in the air and thinking, *This is home. My home.* She drifted off to sleep on the floor, dreaming of couches, and wondering how much longer her friends would let her and the kids stay.

Despite what her family was going through, Angel knew finishing her degree would be essential to keep them moving forward instead of slipping backward. Without a place to study or anyone to babysit, she took the kids to McDonald's, letting them entertain themselves in the PlayPlace while she studied. Studying for a psychology exam, she found herself staring at the color-coded pyramid representing Maslow's hierarchy of needs. She fought back the lump in her throat as she stared at the bottom of the pyramid: food, shelter, clothing. At that moment, that was exactly where she was: at the bottom, meeting the lowest level of requirements for survival—and only barely at that.

Could she dare to think about moving up to a better life when she wasn't even sure they would have a place to live next week? One of the next levels up on the pyramid was love and a sense of belonging. She didn't want her kids to be stuck on the bottom rung of basic survival, eating french fries for lunch and sharing a couch for a bed. She wanted them to be in a position not just to belong and be loved but to give love. She wanted to instill in them the knowledge, the confidence, that they were going to give so much to the world. At the moment, though, what did any of them have to give?

The "esteem" level on the pyramid made her squirm in the yellow plastic chair, knowing she had so far to go. She'd married young. The relationship became abusive. She was able to gain her freedom, but it was a daily struggle to tell herself that the terrible things he'd tried to make her believe about herself were not true, that she was stronger and better than she believed. There was no room to fail, she knew, but watching her children play hide-and-seek on the playground, squealing as they darted away to avoid being tagged, she felt the pressure of what it would take to give them what they deserved.

To get to the top of the pyramid, where you were living out your best self, Maslow said you had to master all the needs below it. Angel knew she had to start where she was, at the bottom. She didn't know how she would get to the top, but she made a silent promise to herself and her kids that she would darn sure learn how.

For Angel, climbing the pyramid was like climbing a real mountain—every now and then tripping and falling backward. The kids were getting older. They weren't puppies anymore that she could bundle up and keep safe with the promise of a bedtime story. And they could no longer impose on friends. They needed a place with privacy, with space to grow and think, a place where they could do their homework without worrying about people breaking into their apartment.

They moved into a one-bedroom apartment, but it was too small, and it wasn't safe for the kids to play outside. She came up with a plan to solve this daily problem. She was not going to let their living situation keep them from being a loving family unit. Where could her family go and what could they do together outside the house? They had long ago outgrown the McDonald's PlayPlace. There was no money for any kind of entertainment for a family of five. The movies were out, going to a ball game was out, going to museums was out, going to restaurants was out.

Angel's solution was for them to volunteer. Doing community service quickly became their favorite family pastime. They volunteered at homeless shelters, the children's hospital, park cleanups, back-to-school clothing drives—they lived for the weekends and helping out at any nonprofit that needed extra hands.

The families who regularly volunteered around Denver made up a tight-knit community all their own, and they welcomed Angel's family with open arms. Angel and her kids made new friends and learned all kinds of skills. One of Angel's daughters volunteered as a counselor at an environmental learning camp for low-income kids. She got to do fly-fishing, snowshoeing, canoeing—things she never would have been able to do otherwise. Best of all, for Angel, was starting to touch that part of the pyramid that was about being able to give of yourself, to show her kids how they could contribute to their community and belong to something outside of themselves, outside of their tiny apartment.

She could see her kids becoming more well rounded and

more confident. Meeting and working with people from different religious, cultural, and educational backgrounds, they were learning to embrace everyone, even people they didn't agree with on every single thing.

And without meaning to, they had the other volunteers fooled. Even though there were times when Angel's kids gobbled up the free food at volunteer sites because they were short on food at home, no one ever guessed that they were anything other than a middle-class family enjoying life. When they were invited to fund-raising galas or volunteer-appreciation parties, Angel took them to Goodwill to buy special outfits. They blended right in with the other partygoers. With few resources, Angel and her kids were enjoying life. What hadn't changed all that much, however, was the constant yo-yo of their housing, and it was about to get a jolt in a direction that Angel never saw coming.

Angel had a good job as a surgical technician. She liked the nurses and doctors she worked with at the hospital. She performed her job well and did whatever she could to learn more. Still, with four children and the high rent around Denver, finding an apartment that was big enough, safe, and affordable was always just beyond her reach. After years of being on a waiting list for a few precious slots, she was finally able to rent a subsidized apartment in a decent neighborhood. Not only that, she was offered a job promotion. A promotion was a good thing, a very good thing—right?

During this same time, Angel and one of her daughters volunteered for Habitat for Humanity for the first time. After only one day, Angel felt empowered by the experience. That morning, they'd had a meet-and-greet with the team they'd be working with. They exchanged names and shook hands. The team members worked alongside each other, sawdust sticking to their sweaty faces and arms. By the end of the day, even more dirty and sweaty, they weren't shaking hands, they were giving hugs. She was energized by the feeling of love that came from all of them working together on the homeowner's dream.

The next day, as she was helping pour the concrete foundation for the house, she caught herself thinking about her own predicament. Her pride in earning her job promotion was all but wiped out under the weight of the reality of what it meant for her family. If she took the promotion, she would no longer qualify for subsidized housing and she would lose her Medicare benefits. Her new position would include health insurance, so that wouldn't be an issue, but her raise in pay would not be enough to cover the rent without the subsidy. The new rent would be almost double what she was now paying. She had to laugh at the absurdity. She wanted that promotion—and not just because her son needed cleats and her daughter needed a dress for prom. She had worked hard. She deserved it. She had stayed positive for so long, but this seemed like a cruel joke: to keep her home, she would have to hold herself back from being successful in her career.

She tucked her conundrum under her hard hat and kept working. Her daughter didn't need to see her worry, and the home she was working on deserved her care and attention. Maybe it wasn't an accident that Angel's community service hobby had brought her to that homesite. It seemed like a sign from above, but it took her a little while to get the message. Finally, after a few weeks of working on the site, it hit her. Maybe she could be a Habitat homeowner. Would she qualify?

There was a lot of paperwork involved just to start the application process, but Angel had seen firsthand how life-changing a Habitat home could be for a family. If she didn't qualify, she would do whatever it took to make it happen and try again. She had to make sure her credit was in good standing. She would need to volunteer at least two hundred hours of what Habitat called sweat equity, working on her own home as well as volunteering on other Habitat homesites. That would be the easy part! She loved volunteering, and now she was doing homebuilding tasks she never even would have attempted in the past. She also had to prove she had enough income to pay the closing costs, monthly mortgage payments, insurance, and maintenance on the home. There would be meetings with Habitat staff and required classes on financial literacy, saving money, credit, home maintenance, insurance, homeowners associations, and even gardening.

But she had been climbing the pyramid a long time. A few more ledges and crevices to conquer would only get her closer to the top. She did all the paperwork. She went to all the interviews. She prayed.

And she was approved! When she found out, she jumped into the classes and the opportunities to volunteer. Education and community service had been the foundation of raising her family, and it seemed right, almost ordained, that they should be at the cornerstone of establishing her own home.

Not only was Angel embarking on the journey to build her own home, she found out it wasn't too late to accept her promotion at work. Her oldest daughter, Rebecca, had earned a full college scholarship, but Angel had worried about how she was going to pay for incidentals for her dorm room and school supplies. Now she took Rebecca to Target. As they walked down the aisle of linens, running their hands over the packages of new sheets in pretty colors, Angel looked Rebecca in the eye, and said, "Get it!" It was the first time she'd ever been able to say that, and it felt like she'd reached the top of that pyramid and was shouting it from the heights.

Taking all of the classes in preparation for starting construction on a home, Angel relished getting to know her classmates. They'd all been through so many of the same struggles, and now they were learning together how to thrive in this next stage of their lives. Angel was thrilled when she learned which homesite she had been approved for, but her excitement was short-lived.

The property was by the airport, and she knew that one of her classmates, a taxi driver with a young family, had been hoping to get it to help further his taxi business. He was disappointed when the lot went to Angel, but he was also happy for his new friend. With this group, good news for one was good news for all. Still, Angel couldn't quite let go of the nagging feeling that the taxi driver really would benefit from that location. She decided to let his family have the lot by the airport. She could wait a little longer. And she was glad she did. The place where she ended up was even better for her family, as it was in a whole neighborhood of Habitat homes, a community of friends who had struggled and worked together to get to this point. Because of her kind gesture, everything had worked out for the best. She was grateful.

With her soon-to-be neighbors, her children, and volunteers by her side, Angel began to build the house of her dreams, and the houses of her neighbors' dreams. They all worked together, pouring concrete, nailing up Sheetrock, putting in windows, painting, and laying sod.

The night before they moved in, Angel couldn't sleep. This time it wasn't because she was on the floor worried about where they would stay the next night. She couldn't sleep out of excitement. Was this really happening? Sure enough, the next day she was standing on her front porch with her new neighbors. They had already established themselves as a close neighborhood, building each other's homes, supporting each other through classes and challenges. Now they would be able to look out for each other, have fun together, enjoy their beautiful dreams together, and feel pride. *We did this! We built this community, this village.*

Angel expected to appreciate her new house, but she didn't expect its effects to be so far-reaching. Now, when she woke up in the morning, she was filled with love and pride. As she went through her day, she naturally expressed that same feeling of love to her children and the rest of her family, her neighbors, co-workers, even strangers. Her beliefs had stayed strong all that time, over all those tough years, but now she was able to put them into action from a new perspective. The view from the top of the pyramid was awesome.

There was one thing missing, though.

Before she bought any other furniture for her new house, she went hunting for the perfect couch. She told the salesperson, "I want the biggest one you've got!" She stood on her front porch, waiting for the delivery truck to bring the couch of her dreams. It came around the corner, and she opened the front door, giddy and ready. The deliverymen carried the massive piece of furniture up the front walk.

"Ma'am, we've got a problem," one of them said, as he put the couch down. "It's not going to fit through this door."

"Just try," she said. "Please!"

They flipped it this way and that. They angled it and tried to wedge it in. They put it down and scratched their heads. Angel was not going to let them put the couch back in the truck. Finally, they took the legs off the couch and the front door off its frame. After a little sweat and an hour of taking things apart and putting them back together, the couch was securely installed at the heart of Angel's new home.

I had the pleasure of helping build Angel's home, and she is such a delightful person. How beautiful that she learned she might qualify for a Habitat home while volunteering on a Habitat homesite. Think about that. You don't have a stable place to live, and yet you're helping someone else build their dream for no other reason than you want to spend time with your children helping the community.

When I think about Angel, I remember that it doesn't matter how busy I am, how much I have on my mind, or what I'm personally feeling is lacking in my life. You don't have to have a lot to give a lot. I remember that when you're a good neighbor to those around you, it lifts your whole community, your whole street, your whole office, and you get to enjoy all the benefits of being part of a community that's on the rise. It's almost like a group of neighbors or co-workers who win the lottery together by going in for a block of tickets. They all put a little bit into the pot, and they all get richer together in the end. Well, not exactly. Contributing to your community is way less risky than the lottery. In fact, it's pretty much a shoo-in for the win every time. Just ask Angel.

3

Empowerment

ONE OF THE forces that sometimes keeps us isolated from each other is what I like to call the "myth of fierce independence." We love to act like we don't need anybody. When we think of other people struggling through something, it makes us feel so big and strong to tell ourselves, "I did it all by myself, so they can, too." But let's face it. None of us did it by ourselves.

Most of us have no idea what true deprivation, true poverty, is really like. Those of us who grew up in comfortable childhood homes don't know what it's like to be unable to sleep because of the cold or to concentrate on homework while we're hungry and there's no food in the house. If your parents read to you when you were a child, you didn't get where you are all by yourself. If someone in your family went to college and told you what it was like, you didn't get there all by yourself. If a teacher, family member, or friend ever recommended you for school, a job, an internship, or some other program, then you didn't get there all by yourself.

For people growing up in real poverty, these seemingly minor aspects of life that positively affect our outcomes are simply not there. The thing is, it's OK to have had these advantages. It's OK if our families and communities have helped us along the way. What a blessing! We just need to spread this support to those unlucky enough to be born without it.

There's no rhyme or reason as to why some of us are born poor, some of us rich, and most of us somewhere in between. But whatever blessings we have been given *through no merit of our own,* due to whatever you want to call it— whether that's luck of the draw or God's grace—we have the responsibility, I believe, to share these gifts with others.

When we empower those among us who haven't had as many opportunities, we're not only sharing our blessings and helping another person. We are doing our small part to make the world full of more people who can then go on to help even more people. And here's the crazy thing about this virtue: even the wealthiest among us who seemingly need nothing can be empowered by empowering others.

Is that confusing? Let me tell you a story. One day I met a young woman named Crystal who was friends with my goddaughter. Crystal didn't know what I did for a living, and we were just having a casual conversation. As we talked, she revealed that when she was young, her mother was in a bad situation. Her mother escaped with Crystal and Crystal's four siblings, but the family was homeless.

I expressed my sorrow and concern, and she said, "But it all changed when I turned thirteen and my mom qualified to buy a Habitat for Humanity house." Well, of course I was melting. I hadn't been expecting to hear that, and I'm sure you know that funny, almost eerie feeling when you hear a story that speaks to you when you need it the most.

Crystal's mom did everything she could to get herself in good financial standing and was able to buy the house. All five of her children went to college, and she put herself through college as well. Crystal was working as a sign language translator for counselors helping at-risk hearing-impaired youth when she thought, *Hey, I can do this myself!* So while working full-time, she went back to school to work on her master's degree in counseling. Now she's saving with the goal of going back to school for a doctorate.

If Crystal's mother had remained homeless, here's what the statistics predict would have happened to her children. Since every time a child moves, he or she can lose up to a year in school, each one of them would have performed poorly and been tracked as a low achiever. Then that would have been reinforced over time, and the children would have started to believe it. A bright child with as much potential as any other child would now be statistically predicted to fail in school, be malnourished, get sick more often, rely on the emergency room for health care, be more prone to committing crime and going to prison, be qualified for only low-paying jobs, and depend on government assistance for housing, food, and health care.

Here's the other option: with a little empowerment and support, Crystal's mom raises five college graduates who are qualified for decent-paying jobs, who pay taxes, and who have the means to give back to the community. And if any of them have children, then the generations of healthy, successful citizens march on and on. Yes!

I get fired up. The stories of empowerment we witness at Habitat are like jet fuel for me. When you meet people whose trajectory in life has completely changed for the better simply because they have been able to experience the stability of decent housing, you realize the potential that's out there in the world, untapped and waiting to be uncovered in young people all over the globe. And you realize we'd better get to work. If we could empower more children, think of what they could accomplish as adults. We could have a booming population of people who are driven to succeed and empowered to help heal the world.

Think what might happen if a volunteer witnesses first-hand their actions helping a person fulfill potential such as going to college, buying a home, or following a talent to pursue a successful career. That volunteer gets to see that what they did doesn't have a shelf life. Its effects last longer than a day on a homesite—it may create what we call generational change for a family, and thus generational change for that community, and the world.

Consider what might happen in a community when most of the kids go from barely graduating high school to going to college. We see this at Habitat. And if a volunteer gets to see just what can be unlocked from their service, then suddenly they're empowered to serve more and feel more satisfaction doing it.

Is it wrong to feel good about helping someone? Certainly not. And that's one of the main messages of this book. It's OK to be empowered by empowering others to pursue their dreams. It's OK to look at yourself, at others, and at the world and see what's possible and get super excited about making it a better place for all of us.

If you're still wondering if it wouldn't be better if people were left to succeed on their own with no help from anybody—if you still think it counts more when you do it *all by yourself*—read these stories. See what happens when people whom society predicted would be a drain on community resources got just a little bit of help. The people in these stories are my heroes. They make me ask myself: If I had been born in the same circumstances they were, would I have made it?

You'll know the part of this story that broke my heart when you read it.

The Speech

Someone had told him not to worry, to speak from the heart, so Jose had left behind the piece of paper where he'd painstakingly written his speech. Why hadn't he brought it with him just in case? Oh well. It was too late now. He walked up to the podium. The crowd was clapping. He was supposed to talk about his life. He'd been glad to be asked, but now, standing here, he wondered why he'd said yes. He was fifteen years old and had never given a speech before. He looked out at the crowd of people in front of him. He could feel the sweat beading on his forehead in the hot July sun. Or maybe it wasn't the heat making him sweat. He knew he shouldn't be here. It didn't make sense. He was a poor kid with a one-point-something GPA growing up in South Central LA. Did they see something he didn't?

When he and his big sister and brother were little kids growing up in El Salvador, none of them could have ever imagined they would someday be standing here in this crowd. He thought back to their one-room house on a dirt road. At the time it didn't seem weird that their beds were in the same room where they cooked and ate. It was all they knew. And they were the lucky ones. Their house was sturdy, not like the ones made of hay or adobe. They didn't have running water, but they did have a well, the kind of well that was only in storybooks in America, the kind with a bucket tied to a rope. People walked from miles away to ask if they could have some water. His parents always shared, never asking for anything in return. By some miracle the well never dried up.

In some ways it wasn't unlike the childhood of any other kid in any other place. Jose and his friends made up games, rode bikes, and played baseball. He didn't realize that the work his parents put into putting food on the table without running water or indoor plumbing was anything out of the ordinary. He also didn't realize that there were places where families went to sleep at night feeling safe and secure.

No matter how sturdy their walls, there was no shelter from the gunfights between the government soldiers and the antigovernment guerillas. One day Jose and his cousins heard the familiar *pop pop pop*. They flattened themselves against the floor to wait for it to stop, like they always did. But this time his grandfather didn't move. "Abuelo, Abuelo," Jose and his cousins begged, "get down! Get down!" But his grandfather refused. He said he was tired of ducking from bullets in his own home. If a bullet was going to hit him sitting in his chair, then it was going to hit him.

Guerillas would knock on the door and ask the family if they'd seen any soldiers. Soldiers would knock on the door and ask if they'd seen any guerillas. If Jose and his family said the wrong thing they could be killed. And there were plenty of close calls.

Jose's mother and aunt would have to cook for whoever

was at the door, whether it was soldiers or guerillas. They prayed that the soldiers and the guerillas wouldn't show up at the same time. If they did, they could kill the whole family.

Now, standing on this stage in Southern California, he felt safe, but still, he was scared. Anyone would have been nervous with this crowd. He told himself not to mess up.

"Thank you for coming," he said into the microphone. Hundreds of people were standing in front of the platform, and they looked up at him with kind faces, waiting, leaning forward so they wouldn't miss what he was going to say. He didn't know any of these people other than his parents and siblings. There were TV cameras and newspaper reporters—and former president Jimmy Carter and Mrs. Carter. He looked over at them. Even they were watching him and waiting to hear what he'd say. No pressure.

They were here as part of the Habitat for Humanity Carter Work Project. They and 1,500 volunteers from thirty-nine states and five countries were doing a building blitz of twenty-one houses, and one of those houses belonged to Jose and his family.

They had settled in the South Central Los Angeles neighborhood of Watts. His father worked in the maintenance department at the University of Southern California. His mother worked as a housekeeper and babysitter. She commuted two hours each way to the side of town that barely knew Watts existed. They lived on the second floor of an apartment building. Their neighbors included gang members. The family had traded one kind of fear for another. When Jose wanted to go outside to ride his bike, he would watch out the window, and when the gang members walked around the corner, that was his moment. He flew through the door, ran down the stairs, grabbed his bike, and rode off, making sure to be back by dark.

So when his parents found out they qualified to build and buy a Habitat house, he couldn't wait to go with them to check out the lot. He climbed into the backseat of the car. His parents were happier than he'd ever seen them, and he soaked up that feeling. His parents' happiness wasn't something he usually thought of. They spent every day working hard, and he spent every day at school, and life went on. This was something new. And painfully short-lived.

One minute he was feeling like they were a family of means on a Sunday drive, and the next minute he was back in a bad neighborhood with a sinking feeling in his gut.

His father stopped the car in front of an abandoned field with an old railroad track running through it, overgrown with weeds and littered with trash.

"Are you sure this is the right address?" his mother asked.

His father nodded.

It was dark and deserted. There were no streetlights.

His mother started to cry. Jose never saw her cry.

"I don't like this," she said. "I don't want to worry about

my children getting shot. Is this any better than where we are now?"

His father's jaw was set. Jose could tell he was thinking hard.

"This may be our only opportunity," his father said. "If we say no to this, we may not get another chance to buy a house. This is going to be good for us."

"It's not what I was hoping for," his mother said.

"I know, I know."

They drove off, his parents deep in thought. Jose sank into the backseat, wishing he wasn't there. His parents had always shielded him and his siblings from the effects of poverty the best they could. They had always worked hard and worn a brave face. They had left their family and homeland to try for something better, only to continue to work hard without making it out of poverty.

He knew all of this, but he had never witnessed first-hand how difficult their decisions had been, how hard his parents had agonized over what was best for him and his brother and sister. They had risked everything time and time again to show Jose and his brother and sister what life could be like. Now, seeing the way his father wanted so badly for his mother to be happy made him feel almost queasy. He wished he could help them. Would he ever be in a position where he could? Where he could help anyone? It seemed doubtful. He tried to fall asleep in the backseat and forget it.

That car ride had only been a few months before. The

place they had stopped and his mother had cried was only steps from the platform where he now stood. He was only a few months older, but he felt like he was turning into a completely different person. He was supposed to talk about what this opportunity was like for him and his family, but it suddenly dawned on him that he was only now, in this very moment, understanding what it all really meant.

He looked at his parents. He saw pride in their eyes seeing him up there representing the family. He thought about being in the car that night and how his parents had decided to take a chance so that they could buy a home and get their family one step further out of the poverty they had all been born into.

Their dream to own a home was coming true—and not because it was the answer to a prayer or a wish but because, he now realized, his parents had yet again taken one more hard step forward. He looked down at his hands on the podium. He couldn't keep his eyes on his parents because the emotions there were so strong, and these were new emotions he had never faced before. He knew if he thanked his parents, he would break down.

He looked to the crowd and said instead, "Thank you, Jimmy Carter, for building us a house." The crowd laughed, and he smiled, relieved to be saying something, anything, good. He wanted so badly to do a good job. To make his parents proud, to not embarrass them in front of the president and all these people.

What he wanted to say next was how hard it was for

people without a lot of means to find a way to a better life, but what hit him instead was another realization. And it would change him forever.

As he looked out at the crowd of people looking back at him, he realized his life was about to change not just because they were buying a house but because, thanks to his parents and the people in front of him, he could see a bigger picture of life for the first time. He had traveled three thousand miles from El Salvador to California. He lived in the second-largest city in the United States, but until this moment he'd never felt part of the world.

He knew that most of the people in the audience, other than the other Habitat homeowners, had never experienced real poverty. The people out there who wanted to listen to him, to help build a house for him, had no idea what it was like to feel as if the world didn't want you, didn't value you.

He knew he needed to get his speech back on track, so he began to thank Habitat, but he broke down crying and couldn't get the words out. When he looked up to try again, he saw that a lot of people in the crowd were crying, too. What was happening for him and his family was becoming real for the people in the audience. These volunteers suddenly understood that they weren't just building houses or even just changing a community. They were actually changing a person's, this person's, life. He couldn't continue.

The crowd cheered and clapped, many of them still overcome with emotion. Jose walked off the platform to his parents. President Carter and Mrs. Carter walked up. Mrs. Carter gave him a hug. And then President Carter pulled him close and put a hand on his shoulder. "It's kids like you that make Rosalynn and me proud to do what we do. You give us a reason to continue. I'm proud of you, son."

He hadn't been able to do much work on his family's house because of age restrictions, but he had helped out where he could. The first thing the volunteers had done was measure out plots and pour foundations, and the effect was as if they had rolled out a beautiful carpet over a dirty old floor. The change in the setting was immediate. The tone had been set for something special. He couldn't believe the almost instant transformation of the neglected old field that had brought his mother to tears. It was as if just by their presence, the volunteers had changed the energy of the place.

Jose still didn't understand why hundreds of people would come here, to South Central, to help build houses for people they didn't know. It had blown his mind when he figured out that they weren't even getting paid! They were working their butts off for nothing in return. And they were smiling about it! They were high-fiving each other and hugging. Some people were only supposed to volunteer a few days, but when they went back to work they were thinking about what was going on at the Habitat site and took off more days to go back. It just didn't make sense.

People from around the city who saw or heard what was happening jumped in and volunteered, too. Neighbors sat on the ground for hours to watch the progress. They couldn't believe what they were seeing. His own parents were acting different. Picking up their hammers to run out the door in the morning, they were like kids going out to play.

Feeling the wave of love the volunteers had put out when he gave the speech filled his heart with a sense of connection to the world and hope for the future. President Carter had said he was proud of him, and he wanted to live up to that. So when the president spoke to the group later that week, Jose was listening.

"People are so concerned with trying to change the world," President Carter said, "when in reality, what you have to do is change the life of one person so that person can change the life of another person. And *that* person is going to change another person. And all of a sudden you have a domino effect of people changing lives. That's how you change the world."

The kindness of the volunteers had changed this one person—they had changed Jose. Now it was up to him to change someone else's life. But how would he ever be able to change another person's life when he could barely give a speech?

When the week of the building blitz was over, he worried things might go back to normal. Instead, his family and his new neighborhood created a new normal for themselves. Having seen people help strangers for nothing in return had changed the way they saw other people. It empowered them the same way it had empowered him to feel like somebody.

Soon other people from Watts wanted to be part of it. With the new grass and the new homes, people from around South Central would drive by and slow down just because they felt safe there.

Jose loved coming home after school. There was no more dodging gangs. There was no more crowded apartment with his parents sleeping on a pullout sofa. He would never get tired of finally being able to say to his classmates, "You guys want to come over to my place?"

His father had been raised to be humble, to never brag or act too proud. But he could not disguise the pleasure it gave him that he and his wife could provide for their family a home that truly belonged to them. He looked for excuses to touch up the paint on the walls, make a repair, or work in the yard. And nobody was going to tell them they had to move. Nobody was going to raise the rent. Every penny they put into the home was part of making it theirs forever.

They felt safe and secure for the first time in their lives.

Jose went from failing almost every high school class to graduating with honors, and he was proud to be able to build on what his parents had provided for him and plan to become his family's first college graduate. It looked like he was going to be able to fulfill this next part of his American dream without a hitch. But dreams sometimes take an unexpected turn.

It was his sophomore year at California State University, Northridge. Things were going well. He had a part-time job at a bank, he was making good grades, and he blended into college like a guy who'd come from a long line of college graduates. But then the weirdest thing started happening. When he was sitting in class, he had a hard time seeing what the teacher was putting on the whiteboard. Back in his dorm, trying to read his textbooks was even worse. He was way too young for his eyesight to be going bad. He tried to pretend it wasn't happening.

It turned out he had developed keratoconus, a condition that would require a corneal transplant. He was used to setbacks, growing up the way he had, but these were supposed to be the best years of his life. He had already accomplished more than what most people expected of a kid from Watts. He was on a path to great things. Would this knock him off that path for good? Would all that he had worked for and all that he had overcome be for nothing? It would have been a great ending for his story to graduate from college—he'd counted on it. Now, without that happy ending, he felt lost.

He had some savings from work, and again his dream took an unexpected turn. He knew buying a bookstore when he could barely see, much less read a book, was not the obvious next move, but when the store came up for sale, it spoke to something inside him. Sure enough, it became a gathering place for the community. He wasn't selling that many books, but he was getting back in touch with that connection with the world he'd made that day years ago. Listening to his customers and getting to know them took his mind off his own problems. He wasn't an amazing guitar player, but he began giving guitar lessons to kids. Sharing the joy of music had a healing effect. Even though the store was struggling financially, he was beginning to feel like part of the world again.

When he eventually closed the bookstore, he wasn't sorry he'd bought it. He was thankful for the way it had helped provide human connection when he needed it most. It was almost as if he'd had to take care of that spiritual side of himself before he could move on. And with some timely divine intervention, he soon had a corneal transplant, a new job at the bank, and, for the moment, security.

He settled into a nice routine. It felt satisfying to finish a day of work knowing he had earned a good paycheck and was doing a good job. He was even able to buy a house across the street from his parents, and then another one down the street so that he could earn some rental income. His American dream was back on track. So why did he feel like something was missing?

He tried to push it aside, but he couldn't help feeling a desire to do something where he could express himself a little more, talk with people, and connect with the community. But he knew he had come dangerously close to losing his financial stability before, and for someone who grew up in poverty, security was everything.

He'd stayed in touch with Habitat, and whenever they asked he spoke at events, telling his family's story. Everybody always wanted to know about "the speech." Had he really cried? What had President Carter told him? After one of these events, a man came up and told him he felt a connection to his story. The company he worked for developed affordable housing. Would Jose be interested in applying for a job with them?

By now he'd been at the bank for years. He considered it his career. But after a meeting about the affordable housing job, he felt something even more powerful than security for himself. He felt that old elusive spark he'd first experienced that day on the podium, that feeling of a connection and shared purpose to help make the world a better place.

The job would not be like anything he had ever done before. He had no experience or training in the field. But the man had sensed something in Jose's words and his story that told him he would be perfect for the job. Still, this job might be even more than Jose had bargained for. As the property manager for a Section 8 independent living community for senior citizens, he would be handling maintenance, managing paperwork, planning activities, and basically making sure the residents were happy, healthy, and doing well. Not a short list of daily responsibilities.

Asking himself whether he was making the biggest

mistake of his life, he rented out his house and moved in with about a hundred senior citizens, all of Chinese descent. It didn't take long for him to get his answer.

The residents fell in love with their new Latino *sunzi,* "grandson." He surprised them one day by singing them a song in Mandarin he'd secretly been practicing for weeks. The joy on their faces as he sang for them melted whatever doubts he'd had. He had found his calling.

He started up a Karaoke Night, a Bingo Night, and Tai Chi for the residents. He felt like he was finally doing what God had intended him to do. He was the luckiest *sunzi* in the world because he got to make a living talking to people, listening to their stories, asking them how they were doing, being a part of their community, their family. The residents' kindness and love brought out the kindness and love in himself. And all because his story had made a connection.

And this wasn't the only time that happened.

In 2007, twelve years after the Carter Work Project had built the twenty-one houses in his neighborhood, they went back to Los Angeles to build another round of houses. Jose volunteered for the week. During the lunch break one day, he was looking for a place to sit down to eat. The only available seat was next to a couple who looked so exhausted he thought they might fall asleep at the table. He didn't want to bother them, but he needed to eat quickly and get back to work.

"Mind if I sit here?" he asked the tired man.

"Of course," the man said. He pulled out the chair for Jose. "So what brings you here? What's your connection to Habitat?"

"Well," Jose said, "my family's house was one of the homes they built last time they were here in 1995."

The woman bolted upright in her seat. The color flooded into her previously pale and slack face. "You're not Jose, are you?"

He felt his own face redden now. He was that nervous fifteen-year-old all over again. "Yes, I am."

She stood up. "Can I give you a hug?"

He wasn't going to say no, but he had no idea how she knew him or why she wanted to hug him. He stood up, and she gave him a hug and her husband patted him on the back.

"I want you to know," she said to him, looking him straight in the eye, "that we were there in 1995, and when we heard your speech, it touched our hearts so much that the company my husband works for decided to sponsor a Habitat home every year, and because of what you said, I raise money for Habitat and I always tell your story. Every time I tell your story I get tears in my eyes, and the people listening to me do, too. I want you to know that other people have their own home now because of you. People heard your story and they were so moved they donated money."

Back then, he had wondered if the people in the audience saw something in his fifteen-year-old self he didn't see. They had. They'd seen a boy who loved and honored his parents, who had experienced a difficult childhood, who was proud of his family, who was on the verge of a life full of good things.

Still today, when Jose drives by a rough neighborhood, he likes to stop for a minute and people-watch to remember where he came from. Because of owning the Habitat home, Jose's father was able to retire; he would never have been able to pay rent with only Social Security. Now he and Jose's mother can rest. They can enjoy their home. They can spend time with their grandchildren. I got to spend time with Jose on the second Carter Work Project in Los Angeles, and the way he has inspired so many in the years since that first speech makes all of us at Habitat exceedingly proud.

Antonia was bent on getting an education, but without the street smarts she'd learned from her mother, she might not have made it.

Her Mother's Daughter

Antonia was happy to drive to her hometown of Easton, Maryland, from her new home in Washington, DC, to accompany her mother, Valerie, to this meeting to clear up an issue at her job. As an attorney, Antonia could ask the right questions and make sure Valerie was being treated fairly. She was listening to what was going on when Valerie said, "Well, you know I didn't graduate from high school."

Antonia was shocked. She was transported back to her childhood in Easton and Valerie's often-repeated words: "If you're living in this house, you're going to graduate from high school." It never occurred to Antonia that her mother hadn't done so herself.

Valerie had always talked about how well she'd done in school. She taught Antonia and her brother and sister one of the longest words in the English language: "antidisestablishmentarianism." When she enunciated the word for them, her eyes would sparkle with hints of what other hidden wisdom she possessed. Young Antonia looked at her in awe.

Valerie was strong and smart, and Antonia wanted to make her proud. She promised herself she would do well in school just like Valerie had and would stay out of trouble.

At school, it wasn't always easy for Antonia to listen to the other kids talk about trips they were taking or whatever new pair of shoes they'd just gotten. She and her siblings went without a lot of things, and the other kids didn't hesitate to bully and tease them about it. But she knew she would be OK. Valerie would see to that. She had always taken care of them without asking for help from anybody, without the need for anyone's charity. Still, there were times when Antonia wouldn't have minded if her mother had asked for a little help.

On Christmas Day, instead of playing with new toys or trying on new clothes, the family would go over to an aunt's or a cousin's, and all the children would play together while the adults played cards. Since Christmas presents were usually just a wish, the happiness of the family festivity filled the spot in her child's heart that craved just a little something for Christmas. And what she hadn't found under a tree or in a stocking crystallized itself over the years into a longer-lasting gift than any toy—the lesson that if she wanted things in this life, she was going to have to go and get them herself.

Valerie was an excellent role model in self-reliance, even stubbornly so. She worked hard at blue-collar and service jobs—at factories, in restaurants, doing housekeeping, whatever odds and ends she could find. She lived for each day. A night with food on the table and her children healthy and in school meant success. She would worry about tomorrow tomorrow.

Without any close family in a position to help or a community support system, they were their own little family unit, chugging along from paycheck to paycheck, apartment to apartment. But then an opportunity came along that made Valerie question all of her assumptions, even about herself.

Antonia's sister had a friend who was the first person in their area to buy a Habitat for Humanity home. She told

Valerie that she should apply. Valerie said thank you very much and put the thought away. Whatever kind of scheme it was, it was too good to be true. She could never afford to buy a home. She could hardly make rent.

One of the first steps in the Habitat process was a credit check. Valerie told herself she could go through with that and then the matter would be put to rest. But what Valerie didn't know was that in fact she had a great credit history. The only debt it showed was a single dollar owed from a long-ago hospital visit. Really? This was her? Living day by day, she'd never stopped to think about what she might have going for her, what financial good news she had been building up from her years of hard work and determination not to ask for any help.

Valerie's Habitat sponsor, a volunteer mentor who helped her through the home-buying process, Anne, had nothing in common with Valerie—on the surface. Valerie was a single mom struggling to make ends meet. Anne was from a comfortable background. She and her husband lived in an affluent suburb. Valerie was stunned to experience the way Anne treated her like just another woman, a peer who shared the same concerns—wanting the best for her family and carving out a meaningful place of her own in the world.

One night, Valerie and Antonia and her siblings were eating supper with Anne and her husband at their house on the river. They sat around the big dining room table like a family, discussing college. Antonia mentioned a college she was interested in, but Anne told her to forget about that one. She could do way better than that! Antonia felt herself blush and looked down. She was shy and reserved, unlike her outspoken mother. She was not only pleased by Anne's compliment; she also felt a strange question brewing inside her. If someone saw that kind of potential in her, why had she never seen it in herself? She decided if Anne believed in her, she'd better start believing too.

Valerie believed in her daughter, but having never graduated high school herself, she couldn't picture what Antonia's future might entail. Valerie didn't realize it at the time, but through her own example of self-reliance and hard work, she had played a leading role in creating a confident college-bound scholar hungry for knowledge. There was another, less obvious way that Valerie had given Antonia the wisdom and wherewithal to succeed, but this lesson would take longer to reveal itself—and it would come when Antonia needed it the most.

Antonia was on her own when it came to applying to colleges—making sure she met all the deadlines, that the application fees were paid, recommendations written and collected, and financial aid forms completed and sent in on time. As the first person in her family to go to college, she was having to learn as she went along. Luckily, Valerie had always been one to learn on the fly, and Antonia was able to use that ingenuity to keep pushing toward her dream.

She entered Temple University and during the summer took classes at a community college. One session of summer school, she was short on money and had no idea how she was going to pay for her next two classes, but she used some more of Valerie's live-for-the day problem-solving.

As soon as she finished her final exams in the classes she was taking, she immediately took her heavy armful of textbooks over to the campus bookstore and sold them back for cash. As luck would have it, the bursar's office was upstairs in the same building. She took the cash from selling her textbooks and put it down as a deposit for her next two classes. Crisis averted. She repeated the process the next session, and this time someone in the bursar's office remembered the out-of-breath girl who'd come straight from the bookstore. She was so impressed by the lengths this student was going to to stay in school that she connected Antonia with grant money to help with tuition.

Beyond tuition, there was rent for her apartment, the light bill, food when she had time to eat between studying and her jobs, and all the incidentals no one told you about. When she was about to enter law school at the University of Maryland, a letter went out to all the incoming students letting them know that a particular model of laptop would be required. Antonia didn't have any kind of laptop to begin with. A Habitat education fund chipped in so she would be able to join the class with the right equipment. When it came time to take the bar exam, she had no choice but to ask for a loan, because she had no other way to pay for that final step in her education.

Valerie had been the picture of self-reliance for Antonia

to emulate, but the less obvious gift her mother had passed on to her was the way she had taken down the protective wall she had built around herself and let other people into her life. Even in law school, it was hard sometimes for Antonia to feel a part of things when most of her classmates came from such different backgrounds, but by letting herself be a little vulnerable, by letting people in, she came to find out that not everyone was what she had assumed.

After the meeting where she found out Valerie hadn't graduated from high school, Antonia didn't ask her about it. Their roles had reversed over time. Now, instead of her mother being proud of Antonia, Antonia was proud of her mother.

Poverty can be generational, but empowerment can be, too. For many years, Valerie may have simply been making ends meet, but to Antonia and her siblings she was their smart and strong warrior who relied on no one. And when an opportunity came along, instead of doing what she knew, what she was comfortable with, Valerie had taken a risk and opened herself up to the possibility that there could be a community of people who cared about her and had faith in her. That leap had empowered her as a mother and a woman, and through her courage she had changed the trajectory of her children's lives.

Antonia eagerly picked up the torch. She graduated magna cum laude, completed law school, and is now an attorney who serves as a policy analyst at a federal agency that works to make sure banks, lenders, and other financial organizations treat citizens fairly. Having learned so much from her own difficult journey, she feels blessed to be able to help others who are still struggling avoid the financial traps of poverty.

———————

One thing I'm struck by in these stories is the sacrifices the parents make so their children can take the next step out of poverty. The parents' leaps forward are not always as dramatic as their children's, but often they are much riskier. For Eric, the pressure was on, not just to honor the hard work of his parents but to act on it, to build on it, and take it out into the world.

Start-Up Growth in Immokalee, Florida

Eric Garcia and some of his high school classmates were on a bus back to Immokalee after an afternoon packing meals for people in need. As he watched the orange groves and endless fields of tomatoes flash by, Eric couldn't help but think how some of the students on the bus weren't that far removed from needing the food they'd packed. He knew that the difference between being on this bus and on the old school buses that transported the farmworkers to the fields was a fragile, changeable thing.

He watched from the window as the bent-over workers picked the tomatoes from the chest-high plants, their faces and heads covered by hats, bandanas, and rags to protect them from the blazing sun and the dirt that caked their bodies. Once they filled their red bucket they tossed it—weighing thirty-two pounds—up to a person standing in a truck, who would dump the tomatoes and toss the bucket back to start the process all over again. The rows of plants were never-ending. The closer you thought you were to the end, the farther away it looked. He knew that each person would try their best to pick at least 125 buckets of tomatoes—*two tons*—that day.

He knew this because, like every other kid on this bus, he had parents who had been farmworkers in these very fields. Some parents still were. Some of the kids on the bus had worked alongside their parents. For all of them, the tomato fields were a constant presence, just outside the bus window, just over their shoulder, driving them to stay one step ahead, pushing them not to fail.

As much as they wanted a life away from the fields, the students didn't want to forget where they came from, either. They didn't want to move away and forget the place that had raised them—Immokalee, the Miccosukee word for "my home." The students wanted to honor their parents by doing well in school and maybe even going to college, but how could they do that and at the same time not abandon the place that had nurtured them?

Eric wasn't the only one thinking of all this. The fields they passed for miles on end got the students talking.

There were all those tomatoes, so many that Immokalee produced 90 percent of America's wintertime supply. What if they made something out of this produce that was at the heart of Immokalee's identity and used it to give back to the community? That was a good idea, but could the students really make anything happen in Immokalee, where the poverty rate was about 45 percent and the median household income was just over $27,000? Immokalee wasn't known for its start-ups.

Eric's parents had come to Immokalee from Guatemala to pick tomatoes and oranges when they were sixteen and seventeen. In their home country, they'd had to drop out of school after first grade to help support their families. Once they started a family of their own, his father would travel according to the seasons, working as a migrant worker wherever there was a crop to be harvested. He would work a second job in construction when he could. He would eat cheaply and sleep in barely livable conditions so he could send all of his earnings back home to his family in Immokalee.

No matter how poor they were, Eric's parents made sure that he and his siblings had what they needed and that school was their only job. His parents worked hard to qualify for and buy a Habitat home. Every step of the way, his parents had not let the circumstances they were born into keep them from pushing forward and making a better life for their children. If they weren't going to let what they had been through stop them, then who was he to say the kids couldn't turn the idea they'd come up with on the bus into reality?

The students met up to brainstorm. What could they make that people would want to buy? They finally landed on salsa. They used someone's grandmother's recipe and conducted taste test after taste test. Once they felt like they had a product that would sell well and represent the produce and the people of Immokalee, they connected with the 1 by 1 Leadership Foundation, a local nonprofit that would help them with funding and mentoring. They were just a small group of high school kids. Would they be able to bottle the stuff and sell it in a way that would actually raise money, or would this be a glorified lemonade stand?

With the tomato fields over their shoulder, they were used to the pressure of being successful. With their parents working in the fields growing the tomatoes and peppers they would use, they had no excuse not to work as hard as it took to make their dream real. After hundreds of hours of planning, the students had a brand: Taste of Immokalee. And they had a strategy to make the salsa, design and produce the labels, bottle it, market it, sell it at events and shops, and manage the finances and accounting.

As the plans unfolded into reality, the roles for the students shook out. Eric's job was in sales. He was soft-spoken and wasn't sure he had the kind of outgoing personality that would help sell the salsa. But he wasn't doing this to help himself. He steeled himself for his new position and began his rounds, going to grocery stores that had agreed to carry the salsa, talking to the managers and asking them how the salsa was doing. He was surprised to find out that he really liked meeting with the managers. Maybe he could be good at sales.

Eric had always assumed he would become an engineer. It wasn't that engineering was a passion, but he knew it would be a good, solid career. Now he wasn't so sure it was the path for him. One day he was manning the Taste of Immokalee booth at a festival, talking to passersby, handing out samples, and selling bottles of salsa. One of his customers was visiting from New York State. She worked at Cornell University. Impressed by Eric's engaging personality and inspired by the story he told her when she asked him about Taste of Immokalee, she encouraged him to apply to Cornell. She even said she would write him a letter of recommendation. He didn't know if she was really serious, but they exchanged contact information.

In a matter of two years, Taste of Immokalee had gone from being an idea on a bus to filling Eric's head with dreams of the Ivy League and a career in business where he could make connections and form relationships. And it wasn't just Eric. All the Taste of Immokalee students were getting experience in marketing, human resources, and finance that gave them valuable job skills and the confidence to make it in the bigger world outside Immokalee. The start-up business they'd created to raise money for their community wasn't just raising money. With the help of the mentors at the 1 by 1 Foundation, it was training its next generation to become the kind of leaders Immokalee and the world would need.

When it came time to apply to colleges, the woman Eric had met at the booth was true to her word, and the more he talked with her and his other mentors, the more he felt like Cornell, a world away from the hot fields of Immokalee, was the right place for him. He applied, was accepted, and, without the luxury of being able to visit first, enrolled. His parents didn't know what "Ivy League" meant, but they had heard of Harvard, and when he explained that Cornell was in the same group of schools, they beamed with pride.

The workload was like nothing he'd ever experienced, but remembering the tomato fields and those heavy buckets of tomatoes, the rows upon rows of tomatoes to be picked, he persevered. A lot of the kids at Cornell had families and networks to fall back on, but he knew that if he failed he had only the fields to return to.

The fields had haunted the students on the bus since they could remember—spurring them forward but also making them wonder how a place that was in the business of growing food could have so many hungry people barely making ends meet. They also had a deep sense of pride in Immokalee and in the dignity of the farmworkers and their parents' sacrifices. With Taste of Immokalee, they had found a positive way to deal with their complicated relationship with the place they'd come from. They could celebrate their pride in their home while at the same time work to remove the stigma of it being a town of poor, uneducated farmworkers and instead give it the reputation of a growing, rising community of people who worked hard and helped each other.

Taste of Immokalee continues to thrive. It now has hot sauce and barbecue sauce made from local produce and loving hands. And the town of Immokalee continues to grow. Its high school graduation rate increased from 64.7 percent just seven years ago to 91 percent today. Conditions have improved for farmworkers. The town is on the verge of getting a grant to put in new streetlights, sidewalks, and bike lanes. When an economist at Florida Gulf Coast University recently conducted an economic overview of Immokalee, he found that 69 percent of Immokalee business executives surveyed expected economic conditions to improve over the next year, and 57 percent of them planned to increase their investment in their business.

For Eric, those tomato fields will never fade from over his shoulder. They will always stretch out to the far reaches of his mind's horizon, but instead of inspiring fear, they're ever so slowly changing in character, just like the town of Immokalee.

4

Joy

PICTURE THAT PERSON you just love to be around. It's very likely that person is someone who gives joy. A person who lifts you up. Who makes you smile. Brightens a room. They're not necessarily the most outgoing or gregarious, but they're, well, happy in a calm, confident way. And that happiness is magnetic. We want some, too. So what do they have that some of us don't?

When I was in college and grappling with my faith, I noticed some really smart people who could articulate their faith and theology beautifully but had no joy in it. And I noticed other people who were less equipped to articulate their faith but who lived in joy. Did the two have to be mutually exclusive? Who was more inspiring? Who was more fun to be around? To me, authentic faith required moving from head to heart to hands that embrace others, not just talking about faith in an intellectual way.

In this world of bad news, I think we could use a little less articulating and a little more action, a little more living in joy. In my opinion, joy is a choice. Like love, it's not just an emotion you can wait to have happen to you. You have to practice it, act it out, and before you know it, you're experiencing the real thing. One of the easiest ways to develop joy is to practice gratitude. Scientific studies have shown that practicing gratitude in concrete ways such as writing thank-you notes and listing blessings in a journal has been shown to increase mental and physical health, help with sleep, lessen fatigue, and even decrease inflammation.

A few years back, we hosted Harvard-educated happiness researcher and positive psychology expert Shawn Achor to speak at our US affiliate gathering. You may have seen his TED Talk, which has over 19 million views. One of the main concepts he speaks about is turning upside down our typical equation for acquiring happiness. You may think that once you achieve certain things you will become happy, but scientific research shows that when you are happy and positive to begin with, you are more likely to become successful—whether that's getting good grades in school, performing better at work, or forming meaningful relationships. Choosing to be happy and positive doesn't mean sugarcoating the injustices in the world or our own suffering. But it does involve looking around and seeing that the good things really do outnumber the bad things.

For people who don't have a lot, a roof over their heads is something to be thankful for. A pair of shoes. A healthy child. So often we compare ourselves to those who have more than we do—more vacations, nicer cars, bigger houses, better hair. On social media, we're constantly comparing ourselves to others' carefully curated highlight reels. What if instead of comparing ourselves to those who have more, we compared ourselves to those who have less? That gives us quite a lot to be thankful for. This doesn't mean feeling guilty for what we have or feeling sympathy for someone without a lot—it means finding joy in what we have and, when we can, sharing what we have.

It's normal to feel oppressed by the world at times, but if we can get outside of ourselves and see our blessings, we can experience the joy in life and the joy of sharing. We live in the midst of a lot of fear and anger. The world needs some more joy, and it starts with each one of us.

Joy gives us stability that outlasts the unpredictable flow of our emotions. That's why even when things are really tough and we have every logical reason to feel bad, we can still ground ourselves by recognizing everything positive around us.

You can become that person everyone loves to be around, who brings joy to other people. It's a choice that is never too late to make. Even if it's just a matter of smiling more. In one of his speeches, Shawn Achor describes how when we smile or someone smiles at us, our brain releases neurotransmitters such as dopamine, endorphins, and serotonin, flooding our system with a feeling of happiness. Maybe we even get a little addicted to that feeling. And maybe that's a very good thing. Because we don't just help ourselves if we start smiling more. Smiling is scientifically proven to be contagious. Yes, we can infect others with joy.

Long, long ago, I was a competitive rower, a sport that requires endurance and a fair amount of tolerance for pain. Our coach would remind us to smile because smiling takes fewer muscles than frowning (it's true!), so we could save energy by smiling. Smiling also reminded us that what we were doing was fun even if it was hard.

It took a while for my younger self to figure out the intersection of intellect and heart that allowed me to fully commit to following Jesus. The result has been a life of much deeper joy. And over the years, at difficult times, I return to these verses from Philippians 4: "Rejoice in the Lord always; again I will say, Rejoice. Let your gentleness be known to everyone. The Lord is near. Do not worry about anything, but in everything by prayer and supplication with thanksgiving let your requests be made known to God. And the peace of God, which surpasses all understanding, will guard your hearts and your minds in Christ Jesus. Finally, beloved, whatever is true, whatever is honorable, whatever is just, whatever is pure, whatever is pleasing, whatever is commendable, if there is any excellence and if there is anything worthy of praise, think about these things. Keep on doing the things that you have learned and received and heard and seen in me, and the God of peace will be with you."

Whether or not you are of the Christian faith, I hope these lines might inspire you—because surely when you're at a low point, there is *something* to rejoice in, there is something pleasing out there, something commendable, something worthy of praise, even if it's simply the warmth of a dog at your feet, the rush of exertion as you're exercising, a favorite line from a poem, or that person in your life who makes you smile and brings you joy.

All smiles are blessings, but we don't always realize
how long a journey some of them have traveled.

Roots of Joy

Chan Ksor had been told she had a beautiful smile. She didn't know about that, but she couldn't deny she smiled a lot. It was hard not to when she looked at her smart, healthy children or when she heard her husband coming in the front door. What most people didn't know was that it had taken a long time to get her smile back. Her children were a huge part of that, but so was her new home in Charlotte, North Carolina, and in particular her garden. It was almost like a second brood of children—the growing, sprawling leaves, vines, and vegetables reaching toward the sun. Like taking care of her children, the work was a blessing she cherished.

It was easy for Chan to see the blessings around her, and the fact that there had been times in her life when they weren't so easy to see only made her appreciate them more. She knew all too well they could be taken away at a moment's notice. Sometimes she was tempted to be afraid that the new life she and her husband, Y'Thao, had created would be snatched away, but she would not give in to those thoughts. She had learned that fear and worry were a waste of time.

Now she chose to bask in the joy of her blessings for however long they lasted. It was like the peach tree in the backyard. The peaches didn't appear overnight, and once they were ripe, they didn't last long. The tree's presence alone was a blessing, and so was all it brought to her mind and heart.

After a winter of barren gray branches, spring awakened in the tree an almost invisibly slow growth of tiny fuzzy buds followed by delicate pink flowers and fluttering green leaves. With the lengthening days, little green beads began to appear along the branches. So small and so green, the little fruit were like the berries from the coffee trees Chan had tended on her family's farm in Vietnam.

From the age of four, she and her brother had worked on the farm. The cows and the chickens, the mango and guava trees, the black pepper plants, the coffee fields and rice marsh were their world. When they were old enough to go to school, they would go straight to the fields or the marsh afterward. Everybody in the family helped.

The iron-rich red soil was as familiar to their hands as their own bodies. And when Chan had to leave it behind, it was like she had lost an element of herself.

Now she lifted back the showy green leaves of the peach tree. A hint of yellow was barely detectable from the green. She smiled. With the patience of a mother, she would watch and tend and wait.

A few more weeks and the peaches were plumper and showing a touch of pink, so that she couldn't help but think of her own rosy-cheeked children in the garden with her, picking peppers and cucumbers. Her children had inherited a love and skill for working with plants that Chan couldn't have taught them all on her own. She knew their small hands among the vines and leaves had the blood of hundreds of generations of her ancestors warming their nimble fingers.

When Chan and her brother were young, her parents had been sent to prison. As Christians and members of the indigenous people of the Central Highlands of Vietnam, they were persecuted by the Communist government. Chan and her brother tried to keep the farm going for a while, but then they were forced to leave their home, their roots.

Chan went to a refugee camp in Cambodia, only a teenager. Her child's heart missed her parents. Her hands missed that red soil, the hours spent in the fields and marshes where her family had nurtured and grown God's blessings.

The refugee camp had been a season—a season of several years—of despair and waiting. The camp was a scary place, not like the warm, loving network of her family's small village. She would escape in her mind by imagining a new home for herself, a place that was safe, where she didn't have to worry. She prayed to God. It seemed like God didn't hear her in the chaos and noise of the dirty camp. Little did she know that far below her vision or understanding, roots were beginning to germinate in the darkness.

When Chan finally got word that she would be able to leave the camp for a new life in the United States, she wondered if this was the answer to her prayers, if this meant she would finally get to put down roots of her own. At first, it seemed like maybe so. On her flight to the States, she met Y'Thao. And it was yet another blessing when they were resettled into apartments next door to each other. Their marriage was a blessing indeed but putting down deeper roots together didn't seem possible.

Neither she nor Y'Thao spoke English. They needed to find work and earn money. They moved from apartment to apartment in Greensboro, North Carolina, where other refugees had settled. Despite their difficult adjustment to their new life, they were able to welcome their son Kevin into their family. In 2009, the young family moved to Charlotte, and baby son Andy was soon born. The two boys were the blessings Chan and Y'Thao focused on.

Their family of four lived with twelve other people in an apartment. Not only was the apartment crowded, but it leaked. She put Kevin in charge of switching out the bowls to catch the drops of rain. The seventeenth resident of the apartment was a big fat rat whose squeaks and rustling kept Kevin and Andy awake at night.

Chan hardly remembered what it felt like to smile. The family farm was like a long-lost dream. Why had she come so far only for her children to have to live where it was crowded and unsafe? Worry had replaced her hope. It was her constant companion. She and Y'Thao argued. They shouldn't have to live like this. She knew her children could see her anger. She knew it wasn't healthy for them to see her this way. They should have a happy, smiling mother who could show them all the blessings in life. The fact that she couldn't only made her more frustrated.

Now in her garden brimming with eggplant, watermelon, tomatoes, cucumber, squash, chili peppers, lemongrass, and Chinese cabbage, and with her three children around her, she found it hard to understand how in only a few years she had gone from that experience to this. All she could do to make sense of it was to think of it as a long winter that made this miracle season that much sweeter, that much more bountiful.

The garden was not much. It was not big. But it was

enough for them. And in every sense, it had grown from a new village she and her husband had made for themselves. When Chan was expecting her third child, daughter Laura, they were still living in the crowded apartment. One day, she struck up a conversation with another expecting mother in the doctor's waiting room. Eventually, this new friendship led to Y'Thao getting a job with the woman's husband's company installing flagpoles. And this same family told Y'Thao and Chan about Habitat for Humanity.

When Chan's family started their Habitat journey, their future next-door neighbor was on site to help build their new home. The land had once belonged to her family, and they'd had a barn and grown fruits and vegetables on it. Now that family farm was growing homes. She still lived in the home next door, and it wasn't long before Chan's children began calling her Grandma. She helped the family settle in and even helped Chan find a job. Chan and Y'Thao invited her over for outdoor cookouts and suppers and to share the bounty of her garden. And she gave the young family a very special present: the peach tree.

In her garden, Chan sometimes can forget where she is. In some strange twist of fate only God could understand, the red soil of her backyard garden in Charlotte, North Carolina, is almost identical to the red soil of her original homeland. And when her hands and feet are planted in it, and the sound of her children laughing and playing is in the air, and the smell of ripe peaches envelops her, she can't help but smile.

Chan reminds me that there is always something to find joy in. When we asked her what gives her joy, in addition to her family and her garden, she said having a home that is warm, watching her children play in the yard without having to be worried about anything, having a table where her children can do their homework, and her son being able to buy a poster at the school book fair and hang it in his room.

There is plenty of talk about finding joy in "the little things," and I am convinced there is always something to rejoice in, but what if you lived in a place where even the little joys were hard to find?

Waiting for Joy

Waiting was something people were used to in Tajikistan, the poorest country in Central Asia, where for every thousand people, there were only 163 homes. Waiting for the bathroom, waiting for government services, of which there were very few, and waiting for wages to rise above the average of a hundred US dollars per month.

People got tired of waiting.

Over a million people from Tajikistan went to Russia to find work and send money back to their families. That money made up about half of the nation's gross domestic product. Following the collapse of the Soviet Union at the end of 1991, newly independent Tajikistan had erupted into civil war. The war ended after five years, but the economy didn't recover.

The majority of the people leaving to work in Russia were men, and they left behind a world populated mostly by women and children. But how could a society of women take care of itself and its children when its own traditions limited what women could do outside their homes?

For women to meet with men outside their family, for example, to seek advice or to hire someone to help with tasks, was considered taboo. So how could they accomplish alone all the chores and duties usually left to the men? Especially since they had never been taught these skills and had even been discouraged from learning them?

How could women, already responsible for child-rearing, cooking, and keeping house in very dire circumstances, add to their daily lives the tasks of repairing homes, farming, and selling produce or whatever goods they could make? And all without talking to the few men left in their neighborhoods? It was a conundrum with no good answers.

After the latest round of earthquake tremors, Unzi-yamoh Abulhaeva ran her hand down a new crack in the wall of her home. She was almost afraid of pressing too hard and sending the whole house down on top of her, but she needed to feel that it was not shaky, that it would stay strong. The plaster crumbled to dust in her fingers. Her husband sent money when he could from Russia, and she made a small salary teaching at the local school, but her distress wasn't simply a matter of money. Who would be there to help her when a wall collapsed or the roof fell in?

She knew she would have to break tradition and rely on the only person in this world she could. Herself.

She found a spot of land up the hill from her decrepit house and determined that whatever she could build there would be better than the fear she was living with now. She bought building supplies with her meager savings and set them up on the building lot. There was no turning back now. She was giving this all the money and effort she had.

"Oh God," she prayed as she prepared to do what still seemed unthinkable, "let me meet such people that can help me." She had no certainty that she could build a house, but she vowed she would go forward with it anyway.

Impressed by her resolve, her son Foteh and some other relatives pitched in to help her. On the worksite, she was comforted by their presence when they assisted her in laying the foundation. She looked down with satisfaction at the solid ground instead of the shaky, rocky surface her old home was built on. She hadn't been able to sleep wondering if she would be shunned for taking on this project herself. Still, she was willing to endure that if she had to. Now, watching her son and other family members, she felt relief and pride that helped her keep going. But there were some worries that her helpers could not make better.

As they got closer to finishing up the foundation and ready to start on the walls, the diminishing pile of building supplies was a constant reminder that she had to figure something out. She hadn't yet purchased windows, doors, or roofing materials. How would she pay for a roof if she couldn't pay for the materials to finish the walls to hold it up?

Again Unziyamoh prayed for help. There were unfinished homes in her neighborhood that taunted her as she walked past them on her way to school. Some were abandoned and forgotten. But often, a family was living in their new unfinished home without a roof, without windows, without doors or plumbing. At school she tried to keep her concerns hidden away and be a consoling presence for her students. Several of them were living in the kind of unfinished homes that plagued her own thoughts, and yet she knew most of them didn't know anything different.

Tajikistan's vulnerability to earthquakes didn't contribute to a sense of stability. The land was 90 percent mountainous with sharp, craggy peaks that stood like stone fortifications across the country, striking in their beauty but also foreboding in their sheer, uninviting surfaces. The surrounding land was rocky and, with the exception of patches of green grass, almost uniformly beige. In a land of stark, stony desolation, the small things that might bring a little joy were so well hidden that it was all too easy to stop looking for them.

And yet the people in Tajikistan dressed in beautiful bright colors. The women wore floral-print dresses and tied patterned scarves over their hair. They furnished their homes, even humble ones, with vibrant-colored carpets and the most luxurious fabrics they could afford. Tajikistan had once been a lively hub of the legendary trading route known as the Silk Road. Now, when the land proved inhospitable and the politics unstable, the people had every reason to blend in with their rocky surroundings. Instead, they chose to color their world with reds, pinks, golds, deep blues, and purples.

Surely not possible for a people without hope for joy.

Unziyamoh was on the verge of losing hope and running out of money to complete her house. All of her friends and neighbors who had doubted her would be proven right. She could only comfort herself with the knowledge that she had tried. But then a friend at work told her about Habitat for Humanity and how they were helping people with microfinance loans for building new homes. She applied for a small, affordable building loan with an extended repayment period so she could purchase the remaining supplies. She was stunned when she was accepted for the loan.

Here she was, in practical terms a single woman on her own, doing something no one else in her neighborhood had done and something she'd never truly been sure she could do herself. Habitat also gave her advice on which materials to buy and on building methods that would ensure her new house was stable, safe, and warm.

As the walls got higher and her home closer to completion, her neighbors and friends could hardly believe she was accomplishing this—even though they'd watched her with their own eyes as she toiled on the worksite in her long flowered dress, mixing cement and stacking bricks. When they asked her how she had done this all by herself, she was quick to say, "By myself, but not alone." She thanked God for her family, her new home, the strength for this undertaking, and the help he had sent, the prayers he had answered.

The house wasn't large, but for her it was a big thing, a stable place from which she could start to catch a glimpse of those small joyful things—the sunlight coming through the new windowpanes, the velvety caress of the carpets under her bare feet. And maybe even bigger than the house was her new belief in herself.

Sometimes joy surprises us, finding us instead of the other way around.

Don't Let the Tool Belt Fool You

Donna Ricca knew she wanted to help people. She had always wanted that. But so far, she hadn't found just the right way.

She'd wanted to be a teacher, but her college adviser had talked her out of it. When she was a student during the early eighties, there weren't many jobs in elementary education in the area around Summit, New Jersey, where she lived. Used to accepting the advice of those older and wiser, she'd followed the adviser's guidance and instead majored in human communication, with the recommended goal of landing a position in public relations or marketing. It turned out there weren't many jobs in those fields either. But maybe that was a good thing.

She got a job right out of school as a residence care counselor at a home for boys with emotional and behavioral problems. Most had been expelled from school, some had been charged with crimes, and almost all of them had been abandoned as lost causes. These boys weren't what most people had in mind when they said they wanted to work with children, but Donna quickly discovered she liked working with these boys no one wanted around. She thought they were cool. She liked spending time with them. Where other people saw lost causes, she saw hidden potential obscured by layers of neglect and abuse. She knew she wanted to do something in her life that could help these kids and their families.

In her next job as a police officer, she thought she'd be able to do just that, but she quickly found out that by the time the police were called, the blood was already on the floor. If she could only rewind the tape of time back and pause and say, "What's really going on here?" When she went out on calls, she found herself delving into the lives of the victims and the perpetrators. There were reasons why people did what they did, and she couldn't keep from wondering whether if their earlier circumstances had been different, they'd never have been in these situations.

Time after time, she'd tell her supervisor that the people on the scene needed some kind of further intervention. "Ricca," he'd say over the radio, "get in and get out. Your job is to get there, take the report, and pass it on to somebody else." But for Donna, getting in and getting out wasn't enough.

Keeping her day job as an investigator, she started graduate classes in psychology with the hope of becoming a full-time licensed psychologist. Her heart was set on prevention. If only she could get to people earlier in their lives and help them prevent the disasters waiting for them around the corner . . . She was convinced that if somebody had done right by these people when they were children, they wouldn't have gone on to be in residential homes, be sedated, or be labeled as lost causes.

What she didn't think about at the time was how different her own life might have been if as a child she'd gotten some of those building blocks of emotional stability herself, the tools that could help a person weather the storms of life. Because despite her professional success at every job she did, she was still a little bit adrift. She was still searching for a sense of purpose and the feeling that she was helping others. And she was still in search of the joy that would come from doing so.

Donna continued her education, studying for her doctorate. She worked in a men's prison and then one-on-one with patients, and she felt like she was helping people. So why didn't she feel the joy she'd assumed would come with that?

One day in 2011, Barbara, a friend who'd taken Donna to volunteer with her on a Habitat worksite years before, mentioned to Donna that Habitat was doing a build nearby. Remembering how in awe she'd been of the experienced construction volunteers on that previous build, Donna dug up the tool belt Barbara had given her all those years before and that she hadn't touched since. Donna showed up at the site wearing the closest thing to work clothes she had, with the tool belt slung over her shoulder. The supervisor motioned her over, and the next thing she knew he was reading the plans for the house to her and telling her she would be in charge of the volunteer crew showing up that day.

She said, "Whoa, whoa, whoa! I'm really happy to be here, but don't let the tool belt fool you. I don't know much of anything about anything."

He was hearing none of it. "You've got a tool belt, which tells me you know more than most everybody else who's here today." He must have seen the fear in her eyes, because then he slowed down a little and said in a softer voice, "Whatever else you need to know, we'll tell you."

The amount of trust he had in her scared the heck out of Donna. She wished she'd left that tool belt at home. She wasn't a person used to learning on the fly. Her father had been a research chemist. Everything was very measured, very by the book. For her to feel confident doing something, she'd have to think about it, read about it, research it, and then maybe try it *if* she could be absolutely sure she wasn't going to mess up. Every bone in her body told her to sneak away from the site, to stick with what she knew. But this guy was counting on her. She was pulled by her desire to help on one hand and her fear of messing up on the other.

She stayed on the site. She asked questions when she needed to. She found herself encouraging other volunteers even when she had no idea what she was doing herself. She was scared. She was overwhelmed. She was out of her element. And by the end of the day, she was hooked.

She started volunteering more often. She delighted in the physicality of the work. She was like a kid who couldn't wait to get to the playground to climb, dig, and build. She figured out what tools she needed in her tool belt and how to use them.

She learned to let her fear be overtaken by that part of herself that was even bigger, her heart. She noticed that when she ignored her fears and came to the site with an open heart and mind, those with more experience than she had would gladly help.

A crew of longtime volunteers dubbed "the Faithful"

(for their determination to work long hours on the build sites no matter how cold or wet the weather) took her under their wing. One made a special attachment for her tool belt so her hammer sat up at her waist where it belonged, instead of hanging down to her knees because of her petite height. Another mentored her in woodworking and helped her build a tool carrier for her woodworking tools.

Not only was she able to soak up all kinds of skills from different people, she let herself fall into that formerly dark hole of the unknown and learn a little bit on the fly. One supervisor, Tom, told her something she never forgot, a building block she could have used as a child. He said, "It's only a mistake if I can't fix it." When she first heard those words she felt like she'd been hit on the head with a two-by-four. She'd been raised to be fearful of taking chances. *Don't mess up. Don't fail.* She realized that fear of failing had held her back in many facets of her life and had kept her from countless different experiences.

As she became a regular on the worksites supervising volunteer groups, she noticed that whether it was a church group, corporate group, neighborhood group, whatever, some women often stood in the back, not jumping up and down to volunteer for anything. After a while, she got tired of this pattern and started talking to the more reluctant women. What she found stunned her—although it shouldn't have. These women weren't afraid of hitting a finger with a hammer. They were afraid of messing up. They saw Donna in her hard hat and tool belt and they assumed she had always been this way, confident on the site, knowing what to do, how to build.

Donna had to laugh when the women confessed these assumptions to her. "Don't let the tool belt fool you!" she'd say. "I was right where you are now." Then she would tell them about the construction knowledge she'd accumulated by learning from different people over the course of numerous builds, and most especially what Tom had said about it only being a mistake if it couldn't be fixed.

With her doctorate accomplished, Donna spent less time at work and more time volunteering on the build sites. The joy she'd been in search of throughout her career was revealing itself in the strangest of places—a construction site. Beyond helping the homeowners, she was helping the other volunteers, especially the new ones, face their fears, seize the possibilities opening up before them, and make connections with one another and with their own hopes and dreams.

One day, Donna's life came full circle in the Habitat warehouse. The Habitat affiliate had partnered with the same school for boys in crisis where Donna had worked right out of college. She was thrilled by the opportunity to combine her love of working with the troubled boys with everything she'd learned since then on the Habitat sites.

The purpose of this particular collaboration was to help train the boys in construction and woodworking so that when they graduated, they would be able to start a construction trade with some knowledge already in place. It sounded like a perfect match between two organizations devoted to helping people find the possibilities and joy in life. And yet anything but joy felt possible that particular morning.

The task at hand was to build Little Free Library boxes—they looked almost like large birdhouses, and they would be placed in neighborhoods so people could take a book or leave a book. Donna and the other volunteers had all the materials assembled and were ready for the young men when they got there. They weren't far into the initial instructions before one of the boys decided this was a waste of time, and apparently not just for him but for everyone, because he became so disruptive and distracting that the instructors had to ask him to settle down or be sent back to the school.

Donna made her way over to the boy and began working with him side by side on the library box. She tried every trick she knew to no avail, until finally she had to dig into her psychologist's tool belt and get personal.

He was so obviously bright. But he was angry. He was walking around the warehouse with a chip on his shoulder and looking like he wanted to hit something other than the piece of wood that was in front of him. And she sensed that he'd been put through much in his young life that gave him every right to be angry. Working with Habitat was a privilege for the kids, and if he screwed this up, he was going to lose this opportunity to learn something.

She said, "Come on over here a second. We need to have a talk."

Their conversation wasn't anything magical. Donna let him speak, never judging, only listening and nodding. Kids like him were so used to people giving up on them, so used to being in trouble, that they almost made sure it was so, creating a self-fulfilling prophecy. She asked him if that was happening with him. "Is this kind of behavior what you want to be doing, or are you just kinda doing what people expect of you?"

He thought on that for a little bit. Then she asked him, "I'm sure you know what other people expect from you and what people want from you, but what do you want for yourself?"

He thought a little more before he answered. As they discussed what he wanted from life, his tone changed from angry to tentative to almost hopeful, as if he'd seen a glimpse of the possibility that he didn't have to fulfill other people's negative expectations of him, that there was another way, and that some of that was under his control.

Eventually they got back to building the library box. The two worked together, trusting each other because now they knew they shared a sense of possibility—and they poured that sense of possibility into their construction of the box. Rich, the Habitat liaison with the school, later teased Donna that never had he seen so much glue used on such a small amount of wood. But, he added, eight dollars for a bottle of wood glue seemed like a pretty good investment for turning a kid's life around.

Because after that library box project, the young man was like a different person. Instead of being kicked out of the building program, he became one of its leaders. Months later, he served as a crew leader for college volunteers during a house-building blitz. The timing happened to coincide with Ramadan. He was one of the hardest workers despite the fact that he was fasting—no food, no water—through hours of tough physical labor. Instead of pouting and ranting, he was laughing and giggling. The college kids he was supervising had no idea that he was only seventeen. His maturity and skill level on the site had them convinced he was their age. He was leading them.

The more confident he became, the more quickly he was able to learn, and the more he wanted to. One of the senior volunteers took him under his wing and mentored him. The changes in his attitude and the leadership that developed within him were energizing for everyone who came into contact with him. Instead of being the worksite pariah, he was the one everyone wanted to work next to.

Watching him, Donna felt the joy she'd always hoped for, not just for herself but also for this young man. Like her, he had only needed a little time and space to create the life he wanted for himself.

For her part, the construction site was not where Donna ever expected to find her joy. Then again, all those years ago, some voice inside her had told her to hold on to that tool belt.

> *What I learned from Donna's story is that there is joy in taking a risk, even if it means a task or project might not turn out as planned. Donna showed us that approaching tasks with an open heart leads to countless opportunities for joy. By pushing past her fear, Donna found joy, and she also provided it for many others along the way.*

5

Respect

RESPECT FOR PEOPLE of different cultures, races, faiths, and economic backgrounds is not our number-one stated mission at Habitat, and yet it's at the heart of everything we do. We are a Christian organization that considers ourselves "radically inclusive," meaning we don't proselytize and we joyfully work with people of all faiths or no faith and across all social divides.

Through our mission to give people decent places to live, we use the concept of "building" figuratively and literally. We don't just bring people together to build homes; we bring people together to build communities and hope. In some parts of the world, this underlying foundation (we have a hard time resisting building puns) of our mission, to bring people together, is absolutely essential. In fact, in places like Northern Ireland, it pretty much comes first.

When Jenny Williams left her native country as a young woman, determined never to return, a person's name or what football team they cheered for was enough to start a fight in the street—or worse. Literal and figurative walls separated neighborhoods of Catholics and Protestants. Now back home as chief executive of Habitat Northern Ireland, Jenny is able to put her faith in God and humanity into action to break down the barriers still lurking. Today in Northern Ireland, 92.5 percent of social housing remains single identity, meaning subsidized-housing neighborhoods are either completely Catholic or completely Protestant. Only 7 percent of schoolchildren in Northern Ireland attend integrated schools.

Progress is slow, but Jenny feels called to contribute to reconciliation, and through Habitat, she and other members of the community are able to use walls to unite rather than divide. She and I share a favorite quotation from one of my heroes, Archbishop Desmond Tutu, on the power of Habitat: "As the physical walls of the house go up, the invisible walls that separate us as people come tumbling down, and new hope is built in the heart of the community."

It never made sense to Jenny that God and churches could be used to divide rather than unify. Now she sees congregations being part of the change, building together on worksites and leaving behind the concept of "us" versus "them." The poorest communities, however, continue to suffer from the most pernicious division and a lack of hope that keeps people mired in the past.

For Habitat Northern Ireland, a huge part of looking

to the future with new hope is through youth programs. Each year, 120 young people—Catholic, Protestant, and those of no faith, from thirty-nine schools in Northern Ireland—participate in Habitat Youth Builds. They meet throughout the year and do activities together, culminating in a ten-day build in Romania.

Alan Brown has served as the leader for several of the Youth Builds, and one of his favorite moments in the ten-day build is the last night of the trip, when he looks over the crew of exhausted teenagers, all wearing identical green Habitat T-shirts. He says to them, "Think of Northern Ireland as blue. Think of Romania as yellow. When we come from blue and we take on the experience we've had here, we mix in a little of the yellow with the blue and we all become green. But when we go back home, back to the blue, how green you stay is up to you."

It's not always easy for the kids to have this amazing cross-cultural experience with one another and with the Romanian families, then go back home and experience the entrenched division and injustices. Sometimes they feel a little bit like an alien, Alan says, because they've experienced something unique that makes them question the assumptions they've always grown up with.

It's exposure not only to "the other" in terms of Catholic and Protestant but also to the poverty of the families in Romania that adds these new dimensions to their identity and their sense of what "community" really means. To what degree they can take back home with them what they've learned and be part of the change is up to them, but now they have one another.

And if the young people can come together and talk about differences and ask questions and listen to other points of view, they can start to see how those differences are actually less important than they'd always assumed—and the country can move forward, move beyond. These green young people can become active citizens determined to tear down old barriers and build something new together in love.

As you'll read in one of the stories in this chapter, respect for different faiths isn't a given in the United States either, as much as we'd like to think otherwise. Neither is respect for people who don't share our socioeconomic status. Our neighborhoods are becoming more economically segregated every day, and our schools end up reflecting that. We can choose what media we pay attention to, and it's only natural that we choose sources that speak to whatever group we identify with.

As time goes on, as we live our daily lives within those groups, our fellow Americans who don't live like we do, whether by choice or by circumstance, become "the other." We may feel curiosity about them, or sympathy for them, or anger toward them, but we aren't engaged with them. We don't know them on a personal level. We may post a sad or appalling story on social media, but what do we do to get involved? Change is only transformational when it gets into your heart, when it gets personal. If you're interested in breaking down barriers and getting involved with people from different backgrounds, a Habitat worksite is a super-easy place to start, and the stories in this chapter speak to that.

Homeowners who grew up with no indoor plumbing build next to CEOs of Fortune 500 companies. One of our volunteers from LA, Allison Brammer, is a sixty-year-old white woman active in interfaith builds. On any particular day, there's no telling who will show up to work. For example, she recently worked with a group that included herself, an Asian American man in his seventies, and an African American man in his twenties with a criminal justice degree who'd just moved to LA from Atlanta. After a day of working together on second-story scaffolding, the eclectic little group was a well-oiled machine.

People get to learn from one another in countless ways on a Habitat build. For example, Paul Levitt, also from LA, happened to be on a site the same day as an Extreme Frisbee Golf team; he learned a whole lot about a sport he'd never known existed and met people he would never have met in his daily routine. For him, part of the experience on the worksite is dropping his ego and doing something he's never done before. You'd be shocked by how many of our volunteers have almost no construction experience, but we don't mind. In fact, the shared lack of experience is a unifying force among volunteers of all backgrounds. Everyone is starting from that same place of humility.

I think about the humility of being a parent. Parenting doesn't really look that hard, and then you become a parent and find out it *is* hard. You don't have much empathy for parents until you are one. Let's say you're a parent in a two-parent family with a decent income, a good education, a home in a nice neighborhood, and support from your extended family. You can imagine how hard it is for a single parent, even one who has the rest of those benefits. Then you can extrapolate to imagine how challenging it is to be a single parent but without those benefits and without a family support system and without a decent income.

When we can let go of our own perceived challenges and forget ourselves a little bit, we can empathize with others. We can respect their experiences. For me, humility is the starting point of respect. When we think about ourselves less, we have more room to think of others. And when we can put those thoughts for others into real action on a personal level that's face-to-face and not abstract, we develop the kind of understanding and connection that can tear down the invisible walls that separate us.

In each of these stories, the invisible walls come down, but the new hope that gets built sometimes takes a surprising turn. A very personal turn. And I think that makes sense because we talk about "community" and we talk about "shared purpose," and I am obviously a huge proponent of all of that, but if we don't feel it in our own individual heart and gut and tears, then "community" is just a word and "respect" is just a concept.

Talking about respect for people of different backgrounds, I forgot to mention how much fun it is to get outside of our own little world and experience someone else's. It's not just an action of empathy to forget yourself and be open to someone else's experience—it's an action of connection that can truly enrich your life with new friendships and a new sense of belonging to something bigger than yourself. David Rubel, in his children's book *If I Had a Hammer,* wrote about this particular work project in India. It was an inspiring trip for so many Habitat volunteers and supporters. I wanted to share my personal experience there because it was my first Carter Work Project and because it revealed lessons and wisdom I still carry with me.

Bliss in India

During a Jimmy and Rosalynn Carter Work Project, you learn to move quickly, work hard, and expect anything, or so I was told. But in the summer of 2006, I was on my very first Carter Project building blitz, and let's just say nothing could have prepared me for it.

The location chosen for the project, near the town of Lonavala in western India, happened to be very near where President Carter's mother, known as Miss Lillian, had been stationed in 1966 for two years in the Peace Corps—at the age of sixty-eight—so from the start there was a sense of connection to the place for President and Mrs. Carter, and expectations for a successful week were high for all of us.

The Carters, their Secret Service detail, Habitat head of communications Chris Clarke, and I arrived at the guesthouse where we would be staying for the week. Arun, the manager, greeted us warmly. He implored the Carters to let him know if they needed anything at all. He wanted everything to be right for them.

Once we had settled into our rooms and then reconvened in the foyer of the house, Arun heard us discussing the build. He had never heard of Habitat, and he asked us what exactly we were going to be doing. I told him that we and two thousand other volunteers from around the world, including CEOs from several high-profile Indian corporations, were going to be building fifty duplexes—one hundred homes—with low-income families.

Arun spoke perfect English, but he couldn't understand what I was saying.

"You? And President Carter? You're supervising this work?"

"No," I explained, "we're actually building the walls and putting on the roofs." I motioned my hand as if hammering an invisible nail.

"You don't have workers?"

"We are the workers. And we work alongside the people who are going to be living in the homes."

He looked hard at us, and I could only guess what

in his imagination the families looked like. In his world, those people and President Carter and the rest of us relatively well-to-do foreigners must have made very strange partners indeed.

"But why are you doing this?"

"It's what Habitat does. We help people banks typically don't lend to get an affordable loan so they can buy a home that's safe and clean. In fact, with these families, it's the women who scrimped and saved to come up with down payments. They'll be the ones purchasing the homes."

"Women?"

"Yes."

"And what do you get in return?"

I wanted to say, "Nothing . . . and everything," but I wasn't sure how to put that into words for this very nice man struggling to understand.

"We get to help families move into nice homes so they can be healthy and have a better life."

"Hm," he said.

At the opening ceremony of the build week, the Carters were greeted with all the camera flashes and thrilled applause and yells of a crowd welcoming movie stars arriving at the Oscars. The volunteers had come from literally all over the world to help—thirty nations in all, I believe—and the inspiration of President and Mrs. Carter was a huge reason why for a lot of them.

Not all the families we were building with knew

exactly who the Carters were, but they understood they were "important people," and thus their presence was auspicious for the occasion. But these honored guests didn't carry themselves the way the families expected. These VIPs were wearing their own hard hats and tool belts, ready to work.

The first day was a chaotic celebration. Music blared loudly from huge speakers. Dancers performed elaborate routines. Family members placed orange and yellow marigold garlands around the necks of the volunteers and smudged bright red tilaka marks on their foreheads, Hindu traditions to welcome and honor their guests. They also passed around coconuts, considered God's fruit, as an offering and to ask for God's blessing for the new homes. The volunteers were beaming with the energy and activity. Their eyes were wide open, taking it all in. Many of them had come thousands and thousands of miles to be here. They were eager to start working.

Habitat had (and continues to have) support from several Indian and India-based global corporations. CEOs and other representatives from these firms were on hand to participate in the welcoming and the opening ceremonies. They were all for supporting the movement to help low-income families get better housing. What they hadn't realized was that they might want to help with the construction itself, alongside the families.

At first, some of them watched the goings-on with curiosity. They weren't necessarily against doing the work. They just didn't understand the concept. It was hot—I mean, blazing hot—that day. Their confusion was all over their faces. Their clothes were expensive and clean. Their shoes were polished. Their hands were used to signing contracts, not spreading mortar or pushing a wheelbarrow. For a while they watched, maybe not in horror but certainly in surprise.

Seeing President Carter, their honored guest, getting down to work in his blue jeans, however, they could hardly sit idle. They still weren't convinced this project was operating as it should be, but they were willing to join the crowd, if only to save face.

When Rakesh Chitkara, an executive with Dow Chemical India at the time, arrived on the site, he'd assumed it would be more like a photo opportunity for President Carter and the other dignitaries, but when he saw how hard these VIPs were working, he and the other Dow associates who'd come to volunteer jumped right in. They were all surprised by how much fun they had working together, building together as a team.

There was one more thing that would stick with him and his colleagues—the humbling effect of inexperienced upper-income volunteers having to rely on skilled laborers for help. By the end of their first day in this upside-down hierarchy, the volunteers had a new respect for the laborers. Rakesh and the other Dow volunteers went home that night exhausted. Had they actually had fun toiling in the sun? What project might they take on next?

Something I heard President Carter say on that trip in India, and have heard him say many times since, is that one of the things he appreciates most about Habitat is that it provides the opportunity for people of different faiths and income levels to come face-to-face and learn, over the course of several days working side by side on a Habitat build site, that they have so much more in common than they would have ever imagined. They share strong values, have a deep love for their family and their community, and aren't afraid of hard work. For first-time volunteers, it's an eye-opening experience. It certainly was for many of the volunteers in Lonavala.

On President and Mrs. Carter's worksite, I settled into the work of my first building blitz, conscious of doing my best to keep up with President Carter. One side of the duplex would be the home of Sadhiya Sheikh and her husband, Aziz, and the other would belong to Shalini Sathe and her husband, Subhash. The women wore bright yellow sarees, but on their heads they wore the American-style sun hats Habitat had handed out to everyone, with hard hats when necessary. Shalini was pregnant with her second child, and the thought that this baby would get to grow up in this beautiful house we were working on instead of in a shack built from mud and thatch or worse made us all very aware of what we were doing.

On the duplex we were building, I counted twenty-one

different nationalities—just on our one house! We had some interesting guests stop by to help as well, including Brad Pitt, who happened to be nearby with a film project. He came wearing jeans and a baseball cap, and he worked alongside us installing windows on the house just like anybody else. Brad wanted to build without being the center of attention. We respected that, and though a picture of him with President Carter did go viral back in the States, he was able to stay under the radar for the most part. It helped that hardly any of the Indian people knew who he was. The most popular star of the build was Steve Waugh, former captain of the Australian cricket team. Cricket is huge in India.

Over a hundred US Navy sailors helped on the build, too, and got to have their picture taken with Naval Academy graduate and submarine officer President Carter. Indian superstars did their part as well, including former Miss World and Miss India Diana Hayden, actress and celebrity Pooja Bedi, and Bollywood actor John Abraham. There were hundreds of us working and moving, wearing hard hats or the Habitat hats, our faces focused on our work. It was an adrenaline-charged whirlwind.

When we got back to the guesthouse, we had that strange combination of being exhausted and exhilarated at the same time. It took a second for our bodies and voices to slow down and adjust from the happy chaos of the worksite to the quiet serenity of the guesthouse.

"How was it today?" Arun asked us.

My hat was drenched in sweat. My shirt had seen better-smelling days. My work gloves were caked in dried cement and dirt.

"It was awesome," I said.

He looked hard at me.

The next day it was pouring down rain. Arun watched us leave with an expression on his face that said he expected us back shortly. I didn't say so, but I knew he was wrong about that.

Over the years on various workweeks, people have told me how much they want to get to work on President Carter's house, and I always warn them that's an honor that comes with a lot of responsibility. He is extremely focused on the work, and he expects every person on the site to be similarly focused. If he sees you not working, you'll get what plenty of us have gotten: the steely blue-eyed "look" from a former military officer and commander in chief. We often joke during build weeks that it isn't a competition—as long as the Carter house gets finished first! He sets the bar high, and I knew the rain would not be an obstacle to that.

The rain turned the worksite into a mud pit, but we all agreed to decide that it was just the way we liked it. After a while the rain started to ease up, and who did I see coming toward the site but Arun himself. His curiosity had gotten the better of him. I showed him where to go and what we were doing. It wasn't long before he was just another guy on the team who by the end of the day was covered in mud like the rest of us—and that was just the way he liked it.

The mud sure didn't slow down Shalini and Sadhiya. Shalini was Hindu, and Sadhiya was Muslim. These two women didn't seem to give a rip about that, or about the mud, either. They were role models for all of us. The entire community of homes would be owned by women. For lower-income people, this was almost unheard of. The women had taken on whatever extra work they could, in addition to raising their children and feeding their families, to save enough for a down payment on their home, with the help and support of a women's co-op and credit society. Then they had put in hours of sweat equity preparing the homesites themselves before we even got there.

During the week of building, I wasn't certain what Aziz and Subhash thought of their wives being the homeowners, or of the fact that they were laboring alongside them as well as other men. The wives had gotten to know each other through the women's co-op and working together on their sweat equity, but the husbands—one Muslim, one Hindu—were new to each another. During the week, the future neighbors worked on each other's homes, apparently accepting the highly unusual arrangement for the time being.

By the end of the week, the extraordinary circumstances and partnerships were starting to show amazing results. The concrete-block walls were being stuccoed and painted a pleasing shade of maize yellow. The roofs were constructed of orange tile, and the trim and doors of each duplex were painted a different shade of blue, red, or green.

Arun had been so moved by the experience working on the site, he had returned several times during the week. He told me he was surprised by how much fun it was to get muddy.

One group of volunteers that I've never forgotten gives me hope for the future. It was a group of ten youth volunteers, half from Lahore, Pakistan, and half from Mumbai. They were brought together by the Seeds of Peace program, a nonprofit that trains young people in the leadership skills needed to foster reconciliation and coexistence on a local and a global scale. The students' presence together on the site was significant. During the partition of India in 1947, when the two independent nations of Pakistan and India were created, violence erupted as millions of people were uprooted from their homeland and compelled to resettle on "the other side," with Hindus from the new Pakistan forced to move to India and Muslims from India moved to Pakistan. The tension between Pakistani Muslims and Indian Hindus remains to this day.

When I met with the students at the end of the week, all they could talk about was what they had in common—how they looked so similar to one another, dressed practically alike, and spoke a common language. All their lives they had been told about their differences, and now they had experienced firsthand that what they shared was so much more.

The dedication of the conjoined homes of Sadhiya and Aziz and Shalini and Subhash was the highlight of my week. First, we lit incense as an offering. It would purify the new home, and its smoke would carry our prayers for blessings up to God.

Then we broke a coconut, God's fruit, on the threshold. The hard outer shell of the coconut represented our ego and our ignorance. The white inside of the coconut represented inner purity and knowledge. In the Hindu culture, the ego is considered the biggest barrier between us and our personal and spiritual development, so breaking the coconut symbolized smashing our ego so that we could humble ourselves before God and embrace instead the purity and knowledge within us.

Could there have been a more appropriate symbol of that week for all of us—breaking out of our hard ego shells and acknowledging that we all have that shared purity within us? All coconuts pretty much look the same, even if some are a little hairier, some darker, some lighter. Inside, all are pure and sweet and life-giving, truly gifts from God.

Each member of our group shared what had touched them over the week, and we offered prayers for the families from our respective faiths. After the blessings, Aziz put his arm around his new neighbor, Subhash. He said, "You know, we're from different religions. And we're from different castes. But now," and he looked into Subhash's eyes, "we are brothers." There were more than a few tears.

For all of us, the blitz had truly ended in bliss: The strength and independence of a hundred women providing homes for their families. The new respect and understanding where before there had been suspicion and assumptions. The love and sweat of two thousand volunteers for people they'd never met and would probably never meet again except in sweet, pure memories.

What is different, what is "foreign," to each of us can be as distant as many continents or as close as down the street. For me, part of the bliss of Habitat is seeking out those unknown places, whether they be in our hearts and consciousness or out in the world, and finding for ourselves that the human spirit is universal and pays no heed to the imaginary boundaries that we use to define borders.

Even seventy years after the partition of India and the violent process of "sorting" Muslims from Hindus, schoolchildren from both countries hear hateful things about their neighbors. Today, there is increasing tension between Muslims and Hindus in India, which has been a secular democracy since its constitution came into effect following partition. Seeds of Peace continues to work with Indian and Pakistani youth on Habitat builds and other interfaith camps and programs challenging stereotypes and promoting connection, tolerance, understanding, and conflict resolution. The power of young people to look beyond the rhetoric and see each other as brothers and sisters is needed more than ever before in this beautiful, complicated part of the globe. In fact, these are lessons we can all use more of no matter where we are in the world.

———————

The Confucian concept of *xiu qi zhi ping* involves four stages. First, you must educate yourself in the knowledge of love, benevolence, humanity, kindness, and courtesy so your thoughts are sincere and your heart is pure. Only then can you achieve the harmony necessary for the second step—to take care of your family using the principles you've cultivated. Next, with your family cared for as you model what you have learned, you can help lead your country in the right direction. And now, with your family exhibiting the wisdom you've taught them, your country following in these steps as well, you can bring peace to the whole world.

Even in a book about virtues, that's a lot to ask of a Habitat build.

Family in Vietnam

During his service in the Vietnam War in 1967 and 1968, Vic Romback and his crew flew C-130s delivering ammo, food, water, and mail to American troops. Vic's job was load master. The crew was also tasked with transporting the bodies of the war dead. For a twenty-year-old from the Upper Peninsula of Michigan, the experience was life-defining. For years afterward, he made his career not only as a carpenter and builder but also as an advocate for veterans as a veterans service officer for the Vietnam Veterans of America. It was over forty years before he returned to Vietnam on his first Habitat trip. And once he got a chance to build not just houses but also deep connections with the Vietnamese people and the other veterans with him, he was hooked.

His fifth Vietnam Habitat trip was his first to the northern part of the country. It was in Thai Binh, near Hanoi, the capital of Vietnam and the former capital of North Vietnam during the war. As one of the house leaders, Vic stood up the first night of the trip to introduce himself. There were three Vietnamese translators who would be working with the group. Two of the translators were named Minh, a man and a woman who were unrelated, and the third was a woman named Mai. There would also be a crew of paid skilled Vietnamese construction workers.

Among the volunteers were five other Vietnam War veterans; a Vietnamese American businessman and his son; four younger veterans, including Vic's daughter, Cindy; a New York City police officer who'd served during 9/11; and seventeen men and women who weren't veterans but were committed to the mission of the trip, including four there to support their fathers, who had served in Vietnam. It was an interesting mix, no doubt. Vic said, "Here we are right now, approximately thirty separate people. When we leave here, we're going to be the most close-knit family you're ever going to find."

He wasn't just saying platitudes to get the group feeling good. He knew this from experience. And it was an experience that didn't get old. Each group was different. Each family they built homes with was different. Every trip had its unique personality. As Vic looked out at the faces before him, he got that familiar thrill. What would the chemistry of this group be like? What would be the joke they'd repeat over and over again? What moments would they replay in their memories on their long flights home? Who would be the first to cry? They'd all cry by the end, he knew.

He was lost in his giddy anticipation of the days to come when Mr. Minh, one of the translators, stood up and spoke to the group. "Maybe it's best," he said, "while you're here, not to advertise the fact that you're war veterans."

Well, that killed the vibe in the room.

On his previous build trips, in the southern part of the country, Vic and the other vets had been treated extremely kindly and graciously. They had visited Viet Cong cemeteries. They had sat down with members of a Vietnam Veterans Association who were mostly former Viet Cong. The Vietnamese veterans' attitude toward Vic and the American veterans had always been this: *You were a soldier. I was a soldier. We are no longer at war. Why should we still continue to be enemies? I have no animosity toward any of you. You did what you were ordered to do for your country, as I did.*

Maybe the people in the North didn't feel the same way. More than forty years after the end of the war the Vietnamese called "the American War," did they still consider Americans the enemy? Then again, Vic wondered, would he blame them if they did?

After four builds with only good feelings between the American vets and the Vietnamese people, Vic was now a little uneasy. He was worried for the volunteers who were already like family for him, already under his care simply because he'd done this before and he'd been where they were. Some of the American vets were still very fragile—not only the Vietnam War vets but also the young veterans who'd been in combat in Iraq, Afghanistan, or Somalia. Some of them were dealing with PTSD. Others were trying to find a sense of purpose while transitioning into civilian life. It didn't feel quite right to try to cover up who they were—especially because for so many of them, it was essential to why they were here in the first place.

He'd been so moved by his previous experiences of mutual respect, it hadn't occurred to him that this trip might be different. He had hoped the other veterans would find the same sense of healing he'd always felt here. Now he was worried the trip would be reopening old wounds instead.

He wasn't the only one worried that night. His roommate, Jim Lempke, was a Vietnam War veteran from the Upper Peninsula, like Vic. The last time Jim had been on Vietnamese soil, at the end of his tour in the US Army in late 1970, he had left the country with a heavy heart that he had carried with him ever since. He'd had to summon a lot of courage to return and face the people he'd once fought against.

Jim respected Mr. Minh's opinion, but he wasn't ready to give up on the idea that he was back in Vietnam for a purpose. He was going to represent his country and interact with anyone who would make eye contact with him. He and the other veterans had come to make peace, and nothing was going to stop him from spreading that message.

The first morning on the worksite, notions of peace and reconciliation were almost lost in the focus on the grueling work in the hundred-degree heat. The volunteers cut and straightened rebar, made rebar frames, hand-mixed concrete, and hauled bricks, sand, gravel, mortar, and water. The skilled Vietnamese workers mostly kept to themselves, Jim noticed. They probably saw groups come and go, he figured, with no need to get to know them. During the breaks, the workers sat off to the side, drinking tea. Jim tried to communicate with them and asked to take their picture, but they waved him off. Mr. Minh kept to himself during the breaks as well, sitting alone and returning calls on his phone.

A few days into the build, everyone began to settle into a rhythm, and bonds began to form. At first Jim had been a little disappointed that there weren't more Vietnam veterans on the trip, but now the group made sense as it was. The volunteers who had come with no particular connection to the country were working their hearts out on the site, and Jim had become better acquainted with Dang Phan, the Vietnamese American businessman. Dang could converse with the Vietnamese workers, and Jim was a little envious that he was able to connect with them.

Jim asked the translator Ms. Minh if he could meet Ms. Nhuan, the owner of the house they were working on. She was taking care of her infant grandson while younger members of her family put in sweat equity on the homesite. Ms. Minh took Jim next door to a home he had noticed every day walking to the site.

The home belonged to Ms. Nhuan's sister-in-law, Ms. Binh. Hanging from a makeshift canopy were numerous orchids in planters with lush greenery below. Having been a farmer and then a landscape architect specializing in restoration ecology, Jim had long had an eye and an instinct for the connections between people and the landscape. He could hardly believe that after days of walking past this home that had fascinated him, he was getting to go inside.

The lush greenery below the hanging orchids was an example of *hòn non bộ,* a Vietnamese art form similar to Japanese bonsai. The miniature landscapes represented the spirit of the family's ancestors and the islands, mountains, forests, and water of their homeland. The plantings were on the ground and also in concrete trays raised on pedestals at different heights, evoking the terraced hillsides of Vietnam. Small trees were planted in the trays, with winding roots and branches, and if you got lost in the scale of them you could imagine them as grand trees with a massive canopy in a misty forest. Ornamental grasses planted in the trays looked like fields of rice. Tiny lily pads floated on a tray of water, and the water ran through a pipe made out of an old piece of wood into another tray, with the barely perceptible trill of a stream.

In the shade of the tentlike covering of the inner room, birds hung from the support beams in cages, tweeting and singing. Walking into Ms. Binh's home was like finding yourself in an ancient forest—one miraculously contained in a crowded house on a busy little street with the sounds and vibrations of motorcycles buzzing by, music playing from somewhere, children playing, and the worksite construction noise somehow in peaceful alignment.

His conversation with Ms. Binh started off as a friendly exchange of basic information. Ms. Minh was able to translate back and forth questions and answers such as where Jim was from and what family he had. Joining Ms. Binh were Ms. Nhuan, her sister-in-law and the homeowner whose home they were working on, and Ms. Nhuan's sister, Ms. Nu. They expressed their excitement about the new home; right now all of them and their families lived in this one house. When Ms. Nhuan had her own home next door, they could spread out and not all be crowded at Ms. Binh's. They gestured for Jim to sit down, but he said he felt guilty leaving the others to work on the house. "You sit down," they said. "Let the young people work."

Through Ms. Minh, Jim told the women he was honored to be there and that he loved the land, the culture, and the people of their country. "This is not my first trip to Vietnam," he said. He could see them doing the math in their heads—they'd already asked him his age. He showed them a copy of a Polaroid picture from his tour in Vietnam. The original was his dearest memento from the war. Its creases and smudges testified to its almost fifty years as a talisman, a reminder of the burden of grief and responsibility he felt for what he'd witnessed during the war and proof to himself that even then he'd been able to hold on to his humanity, that he'd felt love and respect for the "enemy."

In the photo, twenty-year-old Jim wore a *nón lá,* the traditional cone-shaped Vietnamese "leaf hat." In his lap was a smiling Vietnamese boy who was unable to walk because he had been wounded by a Cobra gunship helicopter. The boy would often come look for Jim and sit in his lap. Three other Vietnamese boys were in the picture, too. One was holding Jim's radio phone, another had his hand on Jim's shoulder, and the third was resting a hand on Jim's head.

Now Jim watched as Ms. Binh studied the picture. He'd showed it to her in hopes of communicating that he had always respected their land and people, in hopes that it would convince her she could trust him. She looked at it for a long time without saying anything. Finally she said, "You look much younger." They all laughed.

The women's lives had not been easy. Ms. Binh had lost her fiancé in the war. Three of her cousins had not returned home from the fighting. As he took in these words from Ms. Binh, Jim couldn't help but think back to images that had haunted him for years, the captured and dead North Vietnamese soldiers and the family pictures that had been removed from the bodies. Was it possible he had crossed paths with the loved ones these women had lost?

Through Ms. Minh, Jim said to Ms. Binh, "I have been sad for fifty years, and many other Americans have, too. I can't change the past." Jim fought back tears from the grief that was as familiar to him as the photo from fifty years before.

Ms. Minh was crying, too, as she translated Ms. Binh's response. "The past is gone," Ms. Binh said, "and we cannot look back with regrets. We must look forward with joy. We know the past, but we must not let it be the cause of sadness and regret." She nodded to show the truth of what she spoke, and tears rolled down her cheeks.

She said she had recently lost her younger brother and was very sad about that. Jim said he was sorry, and almost without thinking he said, "Maybe I could be your brother now?"

She nodded and replied through Ms. Minh that he should now consider her *chi,* his older sister. Then she reached out and took Jim's hands in hers, and with words and tears and eyes and hearts they communicated wishes for one another for a good life in their remaining years.

He walked the short distance from Ms. Binh's back to

the worksite a different man. A brother, where once he had been considered the enemy. His heart felt lighter, and so did his steps. Was this what peace felt like? That elusive treasure he'd lost so early in life?

As he approached the worksite, he was greeted by yet another surprise. The other volunteers had seen him talking with the women next door during their break. Knowing some of his story and seeing the conversation he'd been part of with Ms. Binh, they now clapped, smiled, and went to him with outstretched arms.

And the surprises continued. Dang introduced Jim to the skilled workers he'd tried to connect with earlier in the week. With Dang's help, he talked and joked and shared tea with them. When they were all working together, they interacted more, and the men even asked Jim to take their picture, where before they had rebuffed him. The volunteers had earned the workers' respect.

One night toward the end of the trip, the volunteers assembled in a circle for a Q and A session. Mr. Minh had been asked to read out some questions the Vietnamese Habitat staff had put together for the Vietnam War veterans. The questions were strikingly simple: Why did you come here? How did you get here? How do you feel about our country? How do you feel about the people?

Jim told his story about meeting with the women at Ms. Binh's. Another veteran said, "For fifty years I haven't been able to forgive myself for all the killing I did while I was here in Vietnam. Now, after meeting these nice people, I've started to forgive myself. By the time I get home, maybe the process will be completed." There wasn't a dry eye in the room. Even the three translators were weeping.

Jim asked Ms. Mai why she was crying. She said, "Because it is a miracle you are here." Until now, none of the translators had realized how much the American veterans had carried with them all of those years.

Mr. Minh had been the one holdout to embracing the concept of family on the trip. After his fears about what the translator had said that first night, Vic had concluded there were probably other Vietnamese who felt the way Mr. Minh did, but their team hadn't come into contact with any of them—or at the very least, those they encountered had kept their reservations about the group to themselves. When he thought about it, Vic couldn't help but admit Mr. Minh's bitterness wasn't any different from what many Vietnam veterans and even civilians at home felt. "Why the hell would you want to go help those people?" he'd heard more than once. So he'd come to understand the translator's standoffishness.

After the Q and A, Vic went up to Mr. Minh, who was close to his age. "May I ask you a personal question?"

"Certainly," the translator said.

"Are you a military veteran?"

And he said, "Yes, I'm a veteran of the war."

After that, during the last few days of the build, Vic

noticed a change in Mr. Minh's demeanor. Instead of hanging back and staying out of conversations when his services weren't required, he interacted with the volunteers. He helped them without being asked. During breaks, he sat alongside them instead of sitting alone. He smiled. He listened. He talked with them.

As the work came to an end, Jim was sad to say goodbye. One person in particular that he would miss was Dang. It was Dang who had explained to him the importance of the *hòn non bộ* in honoring their ancestors and their country's landscape, and Dang who had taught him about the Confucian virtue of *xiu qi zhi ping*—educate yourself first; then you can care for your family, then help your country, then, finally, work for world peace.

Dang was one of the original Vietnamese boat people who had made a daring escape during the fall of Saigon at the end of the war. He and his father, mother, and sister escaped on an old cargo boat with other fleeing South Vietnamese on the very day the war ended. They drifted for three days in dire conditions before being rescued by the US Navy. Dang and his family started a new life in the United States. He went to an Ivy League college and became a successful financier and investor. Now, after telling Jim his story, he looked Jim in the eyes and said, "I see that you are suggesting apologies, and I want to tell you that you should not apologize. I am alive and my family is successful because of you and all of the American soldiers. Please don't apologize. Celebrate my freedom and my success. You were fighting for my freedom."

When it was finally time for everyone to go back to their homes on the other side of the world, it was a painful farewell. The way the flight schedules worked, almost everybody was flying out at midnight. They stood on the dark steps of the hotel, hugging and crying.

Vic had been right. The crew had formed a family and would be taking that new love and understanding with them back to their families at home.

Some of the younger combat veterans told Vic they thought that now they could go home and sleep at night.

Jim thought he might be able to find the peace he'd been seeking for almost a lifetime.

If you're in the mood to shed some tears, look for a Habitat Vimeo video online titled "Part of the Change." In it, videographer Ezra Millstein elegantly chronicles Vic's very first Habitat trip to Vietnam. Dang and I know each other from working together years ago. After this trip to Thai Binh, he sent me pictures. He had been waiting years for his son to be old enough to go on a build with him in Vietnam and finally be able to connect to his own past and story. The experience, he told me, had been truly life-changing. He also offered one more bit of translation. He told me that in Vietnamese, Thai Binh means "peace."

———

The Durham, North Carolina, Habitat affiliate has a long history of interfaith builds and activities, and they often invoke that age-old tenet I'll never tire of: "Love thy neighbor." According to Blake Strayhorn, Durham Habitat's executive director, it's not just people from different faiths that find strength in diversity on the Habitat worksites but also those from all sorts of varied backgrounds. Blake remembers one build where little old church ladies worked alongside members of a motorcycle club; the guys wore bandanas and had tattoos and of course rode huge Harley-Davidsons. Everyone got along. There was one particular build, however, when Blake wasn't sure that the work, no matter how healing, would be enough.

Love Thy Neighbor

The morning sky of October 28, 2018, in Durham, North Carolina, was gray and cloudy. *Appropriate,* Durham Habitat executive director Blake Strayhorn thought as he drove the short distance to the build site. Instead of the familiar excitement, today his heart felt heavy. They had scheduled this special build day for a Sunday so that the congregation of Beth El Synagogue could participate. But the day before, a gunman had entered the Tree of Life Synagogue in

Pittsburgh, Pennsylvania, and shot and killed eleven Jewish congregants. With about five minutes to decide, Blake agonized over what he would say to the group gathered for the build. He kept coming back to the conclusion that they should cancel the build day and reschedule.

Hope Hartman, the social action committee chair at Beth El, was excited about the build. The last one she'd worked on was seared in her memory, and not just because it had been so hot. She'd helped erect the walls for the second floor of a family's new home, work the seventy-one-year-old never dreamed she'd be able to do using skills she never knew she had. The experience had been exhilarating, and she couldn't wait to get back out there. Maybe the weather wasn't great, but the temperature was fine. She wasn't going to let the clouds affect her.

And instead of thinking too intensely about what had happened the day before, she was keeping her mind on this day and on the family of Subeyda Asmaeel and Haroun Osman, whose home they would be dedicating. Hope was grateful to Durham Habitat for scheduling a Sunday build since the typical build day was Saturday, the Jewish sabbath. She was looking forward to sharing the experience with other members of Beth El.

It seemed like it was a season of building. Their synagogue was being rebuilt, and in the meantime, the congregation was being housed and holding services at a neighboring church, Trinity Avenue Presbyterian. The church was hosting them rent-free during the construction, which could take as long as two years. For Hope this day felt like part of a beautiful circle that exemplified what was so great about their city and the love they felt for their neighbors. While they were having their own home rebuilt with the help of the Presbyterians, their Jewish congregation was able to help another family, a Muslim family, build a home.

Subeyda and Haroun could hardly contain their excitement that morning. They couldn't wait to go to the dedication ceremony later that day. Subeyda imagined in her mind the new yard where her young ones would be able to play. Living in apartments their entire lives, her children had never been able to do that. Right now they lived in a two-bedroom apartment, and the one bedroom the five children shared was crowded with bunk beds. The three younger children were constantly touching the older girls' belongings. It was hard to keep peace in the small space. She was so happy the new house had five bedrooms.

Haroun worked the night shift as a machine operator and usually slept during the day, but this morning he was too excited to get much sleep. His anticipation and his wife's were tempered, however, by worry for their new friends. In fact, they didn't expect the Jewish congregation to be there—or their dear friend Mike. Mike was the Habitat site supervisor for their home, and through the building process he had become like a member of their family. Subeyda cooked Middle Eastern dishes for him that reminded him of his Jewish grandmother's cooking. Mike had gone beyond what his job required to make their new home special for their family. Their home would be his last Habitat build before moving to Raleigh for a new job. The dedication would be in part a sendoff for him. A welcome-home combined with a heartfelt good-bye—it would be an emotional day. They were going to miss Mike immensely, and now they wondered if he would even be able to make the ceremony.

Blake greeted everyone gathered at the site for the morning build session. He put on his signature duct-tape name tag and invited others to do the same. Seeing the turnout of volunteers, he couldn't cancel. He knew his remarks greeting his Jewish brothers and sisters would set the tone for the day. What words could he possibly put together that would express that as a Christian, he stood by them and was grieving, too, for them and for the fellowship of all human beings? The task felt impossible. Would it be better to say nothing?

They circled up in the Osmans' front yard, which was still a work in progress. "Thank you for coming," he said. "I am so sorry for the tragic violence in Pittsburgh. Let's have a moment of silence."

He knew from experience that working healed wounds faster than talking. In fact, it was his memory of a favorite saying of a hero of his, Worth Lutz, a founder of Durham Habitat, that had convinced him to keep his comments so brief. Worth had been a man of few words. He wore a T-shirt that said, "Preach the gospel at all times. Use words when necessary."

Now, ready to start their day of putting the finishing touches on the Osmans' home, all the volunteers on the site—Jewish and Christian and those of no religious belief—retreated into their own hearts and minds. Their private thoughts might have taken them different places using different words, but for all of them, their purpose and goal for the day was the same: to finish this home and welcome the Osmans to their new life, the Osmans who had never lived in a house before.

It was a simple, focused concept, in contrast to Saturday's tragic events. Before the gunman, Robert Bowers, was arrested, he had murdered eleven people and wounded six others, including four law enforcement officers. "All Jews must die," he said during his attack. Earlier on social media, he'd lashed out at the Hebrew Immigrant Aid Society, a charitable association that since 1881 had worked to help refugees fleeing from persecution resettle in the United States. Bowers claimed the aid society brought "invaders in that kill our people" and stated he couldn't "sit by and watch my people get slaughtered." He'd also posted a photo of three handguns, which he called his "glock family."

Hope wondered what such a person would think of this day. Here they were, a group of Jews and Christians and Muslims working side by side to build a home for Muslim immigrants from Saudi Arabia and Sudan. She didn't dwell on thoughts of Bowers. A madman was not going to keep her from showing love to her neighbors and being a part of the circle that seemed to be arranged by some holy hand. Besides, they had too much to do before the dedication ceremony. She scraped paint off door hinges, cleaned up the driveway, and put down pine straw. The volunteers wanted the home to look beautiful in time for the ceremony so they could properly welcome the Osmans to their new home.

Subeyda and Haroun expected a small crowd for the dedication. Mike and the Jewish volunteers who had become their friends would likely be staying home or gathering with their congregations to mourn what had happened. Since Subeyda and Haroun would not be able to grieve with them in person, they said prayers for them, wishing them peace and sending them thoughts of love and comfort.

So when they arrived at the ceremony, they were shocked to be greeted by the Jewish volunteers and Mike, too, as well as another group of volunteers called Neighbors for Habitat who had been helping build their home since the beginning. The Jewish volunteers weren't just there—they were smiling and clapping, with joy on their faces. Subeyda and Haroun felt tears building behind their eyes as they saw how the volunteers and Mike had put their grief aside to greet them on their special day.

As he and his wife and children joined the large gathering of smiling people, most of them dirty from working on the house and yard, Haroun thought about how they and their Jewish friends would share and feel the pain of the tragedy and the hate behind it together, but together they would also share and feel the joy of this celebration and the love behind it.

He and his wife were not strangers to tragedy—or to finding the joy in life. Haroun and Subeyda were both Nubians, an ancient tribe of people whose civilization had once thrived along the Nile River in what is now northern Sudan and southern Egypt. Theirs was a rich culture stretching back almost five thousand years. Ancient Nubians built stunning pyramids and temples, made powerful warriors as expert archers, created impressive works of art and music, conducted trade along the Nile, and grew wheat, barley, sorghum, and dates. They spoke their own languages, only in more recent history speaking Arabic as well.

The Nubians had become a displaced people. As political lines on maps became countries, and as the ebb and flow of conflict and warring factions carried on around them, and finally as the damming of the Nile in the 1960s resulted in the flooding of a great deal of their homeland, thousands of Nubians were left without a place to call home.

Subeyda's family resettled in Saudi Arabia. Haroun lived on a small island in the middle of the Nile in northern Sudan near the city of Dongola, which had been able to preserve its Nubian roots but was affected by the civil war going on in the southern part of the country. Haroun went to the Sudanese capital, Khartoum, for college and then worked there at an insurance agency, but it wasn't home for him. The war was consuming all of the nation's resources, and besides that, people were being forcibly trained to fight the war whether they believed in the cause or not. It was kill or be killed. When his cousin told him about a program that was giving visas to the United States via a lottery system, he was excited to apply. In six months, his name was chosen. He left behind the place where his ancestors had lived for thousands of years, sad that it could no longer be home for him but cautiously excited to put down new roots.

Twenty-two years later, he and his wife were buying their first home. It had been a long road. They had lost their homeland but were now forging a new path for their family.

Robert Bowers had made his hate loud and clear by his actions. Now this group of neighbors was making their love for one another loud and clear by their actions. What they were doing felt like an antidote to everything Bowers stood for. He had his family of firearms. This community had its family of humanity, in all its colors and languages and faiths.

"Isn't it amazing," Haroun said to everyone, "what happens when you can have Jews and Christians and Muslims all coming together to build homes in our community?"

Yes, Hope thought. This community of neighbors would be stronger for all their beautiful differences. They each had different perspectives, different traditions, and different ideas—what a rich tapestry that could wrap them all in its warm embrace and make a shield against those who chose hate instead of unity.

Hope had been at the groundbreaking ceremony, but she hadn't met Haroun before. Now he came up to her and thanked her. She felt humbled to be involved. She had long been a supporter of Habitat, but it was only in this last year that she had been volunteering on worksites and with her own hands building homes for her neighbors like the Osmans. For her, this building was part of her Jewish identity, her commitment to the concept of *tikkun olam,* "to repair the world." There would always be people out there determined to break things, to sow division, to try to rip apart those healing blankets woven together by love. For her, there was joy in the act of repairing, of weaving things together, of standing side by side with her neighbors to raise up walls that would make houses for those who'd only dreamed of finding a real home. That joy was a gift from God she cherished.

The Tuesday after the dedication ceremony, an interfaith group of Duke University students painted a mural on the East Campus tunnel honoring the victims of the Tree of Life shooting, the congregation, and the city of Pittsburgh. They painted the names of the dead, a Star of David, the Pittsburgh Steelers logo, and a line from a popular contemporary Jewish song: "We must build this world from love."

A few days later, someone vandalized the mural with a

swastika, the third swastika to appear on the Duke campus within the year.

There will always be things to repair in this world. There will always be hurts that need healing. But as long as there are people willing to set about that work with love in their hearts for one another, they will always find a home in each other's embrace, a home that will withstand the dark clouds and the burning sun, that will stand higher than the tallest steeple, shine more radiantly than the brightest temple, and endure longer than the oldest pyramid.

Leviticus 19:34 reads: "You shall treat the stranger who sojourns with you as the native among you, and you shall love him as yourself, for you were strangers in the land of Egypt." Every one of us has been a stranger, at one time or another, even in our own land. Every one of us has sought refuge from some kind of danger, fear, or tragedy, searching for a home that feels safe and warm.

Mike, the Habitat site supervisor who had become like family to the Osmans, had a tradition of painting a message of hope over the front door of every new home during the framing stage of construction. That message would join the other signatures, quotations, and prayers written inside the walls by everyone who worked on the house, surrounding the family in love. After he consulted with Haroun and Subeyda, this was the message Mike painted over their door:

ادخلوها بسلام وامان بقلوب وعقول مطمئنة
ومنشرحة.

"MAY ALL WHO ENTER THIS HOME DO SO IN PEACE,
WITH AN OPEN HEART AND AN OPEN MIND."

*In their five children, Haroun and Subeyda are
nurturing the next generation of open hearts and
minds. Haroun said that the experience with Mike
and the volunteers illustrated for his children the
lesson "Always join those who are doing the good.
It doesn't matter where they are coming from—are
they doing the good?"*

6

Generosity

WHEN PRESIDENT GEORGE H. W. Bush passed away and reporters were reflecting on his legacy, a line from his 1989 inaugural address caught my eye: "I take as my guide the hope of a saint: in crucial things, unity; in important things, diversity; in all things, generosity." Generosity as a virtue is underrated, and yet it's at the heart of almost every person and action we admire. If we can approach situations with a spirit of generosity rather than self-interest, we open up a whole world of opportunities.

Throughout this book, there are stories of people who have so little and yet give without thinking twice. In the poorest of places, you can find the most effusive hospitality. When we share, we start whatever conversation we are having from a place of friendship instead of competing interests. It's very difficult to lash out at someone who has just handed you a cup of tea.

Acts of giving can communicate what words sometimes cannot. With a small amount of effort, generosity can transcend whatever it was we were trying to say or figure out. Generosity, heartfelt or even a little forced, is a powerful balm for the giver and the receiver. It soothes and comforts. It puts us at ease. It's a wonderful starting point for negotiation, reconciliation, and relationships.

When we give our time, resources, and energy, we become less important. We can worry about ourselves less. It's downright freeing.

When we show generosity to another person, we're not only improving their circumstances; we're creating a connection with them and showing them that they are worthy of love and care.

In the case of Anita Stewart, for example, her community at work rallied around her. Anita worked two jobs to stay afloat and get her finances in order so she could purchase a Habitat home. A single mother, she often went hungry so her children wouldn't. Still, she would never let them see her cry. Instead she kept on moving, working toward a better day. She had been the custodian at Mills Park Middle School in Cary, North Carolina, since its founding in 2010, and the school was like home to her. But she had no idea just how much the teachers and staff there thought of her as family.

When she finally qualified to buy a Habitat home after four tries, the teachers and staff at Mills Park were not going to let her go through the challenges of moving out of Section 8 housing and into her new home all by herself. When she underestimated the closing costs, a teacher and one of the cafeteria staff helped put together a GoFundMe page for her. The teacher and assistant principal shared the page, and it wasn't long before the local news found out. Within forty-eight hours, she had reached the amount for her closing costs plus extra to help her buy some things for the home.

Her school family didn't stop there. They volunteered hours and hours in the hot sun on the homesite to help fulfill her sweat equity. That was huge because with her second job, cleaning office buildings at night, making time for the sweat equity was a challenge.

When she finally got to move in, she looked around and soaked it all in. If not for help from her school community, she would still be working on getting there. The way they had supported her showed her that the hard work she put in every day was not for naught. The teachers and staff at school really were her family. She really was loved and appreciated. And that was a good feeling that made her new home even more warm and comforting.

Another aspect of generosity we get to witness at Habitat is the concept of paying forward the generosity you've received. A brother and sister were attending college when their mother, a Habitat homeowner, passed away. The siblings couldn't use their childhood home themselves, and the mortgage was more than they could afford. Instead of selling it, though, they donated the home back to Habitat so that another family could purchase it. They had their reasons.

In the apartment complex where they had lived before moving into the Habitat home as children, there was a playground. They would look longingly at it through the window. Their mother, a single mom who worked two jobs, wouldn't let them play on it because there were people selling and doing drugs there.

When they were trying to figure out what to do with their mother's house, they thought a lot about their childhood. Maybe they could help a kid who couldn't play on the playground in his or her own neighborhood. Maybe they could try to change another family's history the way their history had been positively altered by moving to a Habitat home. They knew it was the right thing to do.

Generosity can help fill in some of the gaps caused by injustice, unfairness, and plain old bad luck. It can start conversations when before there was tension. It can show people we care when they feel uncared for. When we practice this virtue, we are not only helping others but also planting the seeds of generosity for the future. When we help others, others will be in a position to help more, and that's the kind of exponential power that the world needs.

Don't bother telling Boris Henderson about long odds or lost causes.

Open Doors

Though he was a new member of Habitat for Humanity International's board of directors, Boris Henderson had participated in many Habitat builds, and he deeply cherished each one. This build was different. It was his first trip to Southeast Asia, and as he and the other board members slowly bumped down the road to a village outside Phnom Penh, the capital of Cambodia, to work on a home as part of their weeklong meeting, Boris thought about the people sharing the van ride. The group comprised the kind of people you'd expect on a board of directors—current and former CEOs, CFOs, entrepreneurs, and investors from global corporations and organizations. Résumé-wise, Boris fit right in with his business school degree from Wake Forest, undergraduate degree from Davidson College, years in high-level banking and consulting, and his current position in executive leadership at a Charlotte, North Carolina, nonprofit developing affordable housing and working to improve the community's economic outlook. And yet he had to pinch himself.

After his induction onto the international board, his mentor Ed Crutchfield—retired First Union CEO and fellow Davidson alum—and his wife, Barbara, were the first to call Boris to congratulate him. "This is one of your most important achievements and the one we are most proud of," they said, "because you will be in a position to give so much more—not just to your community but to impact the world."

That conversation had been one of the proudest moments in Boris's life. Ed had been his mentor for nearly seventeen years. He'd supported him and guided him. All Ed and his other mentors had ever asked of Boris in return was for him to pay it forward. Boris would rather do anything than disappoint the man who had become like a father to him.

In Cambodia, driving past dwellings along the road that were little more than tacked-together pieces of salvaged tin, bamboo, and plastic tarps, the fact that he really was in a position to impact the world was slowly sinking in. It wasn't just the day of building he silently prayed would make an impact but also the decisions and plans the board would make in hopes of lifting up more people from poverty to a place where they could provide for their families. He knew that despite the most improbable circumstances, it could be done. In the distance he noticed Buddhist temples, shrines, and pagodas along the mountaintop. North Carolina felt far away.

But there was an irony he was savoring. He could remember when he didn't know there was such a thing as houses that had warm running water and an indoor toilet. If he had been born with parents who were wealthy, he probably wouldn't be on this van right now. He wondered if he would have ever truly understood the gift of being able to give if he'd never understood what it felt like to have so very little.

Boris was one of five children. His mother was thirteen years old when she had her first child. Their house was at the end of a bumpy dirt road, a small, spare structure precariously balanced on brick piers. When it was hot in the summer, they spent as much time outside as they could. When it was cold in the winter, they shared a bed to stay warm.

"Nothing good's ever going to come out of that house," people whispered behind his mother's back. As if those whispers were a self-fulfilling prophecy, Boris failed the first grade and began acting out. Whatever innocent hope for the future he'd been born with had been quickly snuffed out. Whatever sense he'd had of being a kid like any other was shattered. He had every reason not to expect much out of life.

When he was eight years old, his family moved to one of the worst neighborhoods in Charlotte, an area outsiders called simply "the Hole." Over a five-year period, their neighborhood was the site of twenty-one murders. Boris shuddered in fear at night hearing the sound of gunshots. But worse than the fear his family lived with and the obvious challenges of poverty was the lack of hope.

Yet it wasn't long before the first of many doors opened in his life. This first one was quite literal—the door to his family's Habitat home when he was eleven years old. The look on his mother's face when she told him and his siblings that she'd qualified to buy a Habitat house was a treasured memory he carried with him. He'd never seen that look on her face before. She was actually smiling. Her expression beamed with joy, hope, and love. If his mother's face could undergo a transformation like that after so many long hours of working and so many years of tired worry, what else might be possible?

Their new home was built in a neighborhood called Optimist Park, an old mill village that had undergone the beginnings of a revitalization in 1987 when President and Mrs. Carter brought the Carter Work Project to town and built fourteen Habitat for Humanity homes. Thanks to that initial push, Habitat was able to build more homes in the neighborhood. Boris would always consider President and Mrs. Carter two of the first guardian angels in his new life. What if they hadn't chosen Charlotte for the build? What if there hadn't been enough resources and support for the Habitat affiliate there to help his mother purchase a home and they'd had to keep on eking out a life in the Hole?

The kids of Optimist Park, who'd all come from neighborhoods like the Hole, would finally get a taste of what optimism really meant. For the families able to purchase homes for the first time, Optimist Park was definitely a move in the right direction. What no one would have guessed is that the kids who grew up there would help move Optimist Park in the right direction as well.

He and the other kids of Optimist Park weren't just experiencing the stability of a nice home for the first time in their lives; they were also being supported by a community for the first time. They played sports together at the nearby Johnston YMCA. A local church sponsored an after-school program where they worked on their homework together. The adults who volunteered there were like family—and they required the best of everyone.

An organization called Communities in Schools provided mentors as well, supporting the kids in everything from reading skills to college visits and summer jobs. The first time Boris ever went to the dentist was through Communities in Schools. The Communities in Schools site coordinator at his high school, Renee Anthony Leak, was another guardian angel for Boris. She was one of the positive people in his life who believed in him, and she had a no-excuse policy. She not only showed him what was possible for him but also nurtured the knowledge, skills, and relationships to help him go after it.

Boris, the ne'er-do-well who'd flunked first grade, was taking advantage of every open door he could find all the way to the prestigious Davidson College, where he would eventually be inducted into the Hall of Fame for football. And he wasn't the only Habitat kid from Optimist Park defying the longest odds. An astonishing number of them, refuting all statistics, went to college and into the military. Boris's best buddy, JR Williams, double-majored at Chapel Hill and went on to Duke for business school. Instead of dozens of kids growing into adults barely managing to get by, the neighborhood was nurturing dozens of kids growing into adults who could contribute to the well-being of their families and their communities.

While Boris was a sophomore at Davidson, he was asked to speak at a meeting of the Communities in Schools board of trustees. Even though Boris was shy, he knew he wouldn't have trouble coming up with what to say; if all he did was make a list of what that organization had done to help him on his journey and the doors it had opened, it would take up all the time allotted for his speech. He poured his heart out about growing up in Optimist Park and how Communities in Schools had been integral to getting him where he was now—playing football and studying at Davidson.

After the speech, one of the Communities in Schools trustees gave him a playful punch on the shoulder and asked him with a wink if he wasn't a little small to be playing defensive lineman. That was how Boris met Ed Crutchfield. Ed was well known in Charlotte as an accomplished businessman, and he gave Boris plenty of career advice over the years, but what Boris soaked up most from Ed's wisdom was the importance he placed on giving back to the community.

Boris watched and learned, and he told himself he would try his best to honor all that Ed and his other guardian angels had given to him by giving of himself in return. As he began to build a career of his own and married and started a family, he found it scary to think what would have happened to him, and to the other Optimist Park kids, if they hadn't had the opportunity of moving into a Habitat home.

Now one of his greatest pleasures was being able to re-create that experience for other kids, the feeling of light and magic as they opened the new door of a Habitat home for their family. He worked on helping open the other magic doors to a better life that had been opened for him, too. He served as a board member at the same YMCA where he and his friends got to learn what it was to be part of a team and to run and laugh and have fun. He coached YMCA basketball and flag football. He volunteered for Communities in Schools and served on its board. He and his best friend from Optimist Park quietly pooled together some of their own money to help fund a college scholarship for a young person from Charlotte who'd grown up in a Habitat home just like they had.

On the way to the build site, it struck him that doors were still opening for him, even in this land far away from Optimist Park. Or was it so far away after all? A few of the friends he'd grown up with there were originally from Cambodia, and he'd told them he was coming on this trip. Now he saw the conditions they had come from. Talk about insurmountable odds. Almost three-quarters of the people in Cambodia lived on less than three dollars a day. Children stayed out of school because their families didn't have money for shoes, uniforms, books, or food for them to take for lunch. Boris thought of his Cambodian friends back home and said another prayer of thanks for Optimist Park.

The build with the Habitat board was a one-day whirl-wind. On the van ride back to the hotel, he thought about the Cambodian family. The family were Buddhists, and for them, the Buddhist virtue of *dana,* giving without expecting anything in return, was the first step in crossing over from the shore of suffering to the shore of happiness and enlightenment. For Boris, that echoed the New Testament verse "From everyone to whom much has been given, much will be required."

There was suffering in Charlotte, North Carolina, and there was suffering in the villages outside Phnom Penh, Cambodia, but there was an even stronger, more magical, more holy universal phenomenon that he marveled at—the human desire to love and help one another.

Boris Henderson is, as far as I know, the first Habitat homebuyer to serve on our international board of directors. His personal humility masks a big heart and a fierce determination to make his community and others better. People like Boris are why we build.

The next story is a reminder that you don't have to do something splashy to do something very, very big.

Parting Gifts

Sixty-five-year-old Bob Karlstrand was a quiet guy. For thirty-eight years, he lived in the same picture-perfect house in Maple Grove, Minnesota, that he'd bought brand-new in 1976 for $37,900. He saved his money and lived frugally so he could retire early at the age of fifty from his job as an office manager at an insurance agency. An only child, he took care of his parents when each of them got ill. His father died in 1983 and his mother in 1999. He never married, never had children. He had no phone, no TV, no computer. He lived a quiet life and mostly kept to himself, and yet during his last months on earth he touched almost everyone he came into contact with. For some of those people, whom he'd never met before, he changed their lives.

Mike Nelson, the director of land development for Twin Cities Habitat, was at his desk one day when the receptionist said there was a gentleman in the lobby who was interested in donating some property. Mike fielded these inquiries fairly often, but rarely in person without some other kind of contact first. Most people wanted to know about tax breaks.

He went downstairs, and standing in the lobby was a tall man, well over six feet. He was bald and had a white beard almost down to his chest. His eyes were a piercing blue, and they were lively and warm. The man introduced himself as Bob Karlstrand, and they shook hands and sat down.

"I have a house in Maple Grove, Minnesota," Bob said. "And I have a terminal illness and I'd like to talk to you about giving the house to your organization."

Bob had put his situation so matter-of-factly that it took Mike aback. Not only that, but the guy looked healthy, and he had a calm demeanor. Mike wasn't at all sure he himself would have been so sedate about it, so at peace with his fate, if he had only a few months to live. But Mike would soon learn that peace was at the heart of everything Bob did. He had one request of Habitat if he donated his house. "Could it go to a veteran?"

Bob had enlisted in the US Air Force in 1967 right out of high school at the age of seventeen. He'd wanted to join the navy, but they said he was too young. From U-Tapao Air Base in Thailand, he worked on a crew handling the logistics for B-52 bombers. They flew thirty missions a day, so it was a 24/7 job. During his time off, he was able to escape the complexities and stresses of war by traveling around Thailand, and through those journeys he found a love for travel that became a passion.

When he finished his service, he went to the University of Minnesota on the GI Bill and graduated in 1973. From there, he got a job at the insurance agency and bought his home in Maple Grove. "It's a little outdated," he told Mike, "but it's a good house, and I think someone could use it."

When Mike went to visit Bob's home, he felt like he was walking into his own home thirty years before. What was so striking wasn't just the similarity in floorplans but that nothing had been changed since Bob had bought it. It still had the same burnt-orange kitchen countertops and harvest-gold appliances. On the counter was a radio from the 1970s in working order that looked as if it had just come out of the box.

As Mike got to know Bob, it all seemed to fit. His house was good enough for him the way it was. It worked. It was shelter. He didn't need anything fancy. He didn't need any creature comforts. What he saved his money for was golf and travel. He'd made it a goal to play every golf course in Minnesota and gotten pretty close. He had the scorecards from the 535 courses he'd played.

Over the years he'd traveled extensively in Peru, Cambodia, Paraguay, Brazil, Argentina, Guatemala, and China, spending weeks and sometimes months hiking or on buses, and volunteering in Guatemala. Renewing his passport was one of the few markers of time in his retired life, but this year when it had come up again he had not renewed it.

He'd been diagnosed with colon cancer that had spread to his lungs. The cancer treatment had damaged his lungs to the point that they were failing. He was an active, healthy man. He walked three miles to the library (and three miles back) to use the phone and computer and check out books several times a week. There were people in town who only knew him from seeing him on his regular walks. "There's Bob!" they would say.

Now it was getting harder for him to walk and breathe. He saved his energy for the very important task of giving away everything he owned before he passed from this world to the next. It was a task he took to with love and cheer in his twinkling blue eyes. And it was a task that was going to take a lot of time and thought.

Other than his scorecards, what was in his house was all the things from his childhood that his mother had kept and that he'd never thrown away: board games, toys, a cradle, family photographs, letters he'd written his mother when he was in the service. He wanted to give away any item in the house anyone could possibly use. He liked seeing who got what and knowing where it went, but he wasn't sad to see anything go. "In the end," he said with the wistfulness of a man who knows, "it's only material things. I've had a good life, so I can't complain at all. I find myself very lucky."

As Habitat worked on finding a veteran who would be a good fit to purchase Bob's home, Bob continued his task of giving things away. One day, he showed up at the University of Minnesota nursing school. He'd met a lot of wonderful nurses at the VA hospital during the last few years, and he'd always remembered the care the hospice nurses had shown his parents years before. He admired the work of nurses so much and felt such an appreciation for their skills and care that he said he wanted to "help a little bit." And help he did. Bob had only spent a fraction of what he'd saved. That day he gave a million dollars to the nursing school for an endowed scholarship. He even got to meet the first six recipients.

One nursing student in particular told him the scholarship was an answer to a prayer—that she and her husband didn't know how they were going to pay for her tuition plus child care. The student told Bob she was thinking of specializing in end-of-life care. Bob didn't need that kind of care just yet, but he knew it was coming soon.

Matt Haugen, communications manager at Twin Cities Habitat, asked Bob if it was OK if he wrote a story about how he was donating his home. Bob demurred, of course, but when Matt said the purpose was to drum up support for Habitat's veterans initiatives, he agreed. Matt had no idea what he was starting. It wasn't long before the story of Bob and his mission to give away everything he owned, big and small, made its way to the local news, social media, and even national publications such as *USA Today*. Shortly after the news broke, Bob realized he could no longer live in his house but instead needed assisted living.

When she got the news that she had been chosen to buy Bob's home, navy veteran Bonnie and her teenage grandson were living in a small apartment. A new home would give them space to enjoy each other's company rather than be crammed together. It would give them a yard and a neighborhood. Bonnie had suffered a back injury and used a wheelchair to get around. Nevertheless, she did her sweat equity on the renovations to Bob's home. Lynda Bouley, the Habitat site supervisor, taught her construction skills Bonnie had never thought she'd have, including using power tools. Bonnie's little Chihuahua, Pepsi, was a constant presence who kept the worksite laughing. "Watch out for Pepsi" was a refrain as the crew of volunteers worked.

The regular crew of Habitat volunteers always got satisfaction from their work, but working on the home where Bob had made a life for himself and getting it ready for Bonnie and her grandson to make a new life gave them even more satisfaction than usual. Still, the building crew and the Habitat staff couldn't help but wonder if Bob would be around to see his wish for a veteran to move into his home come true.

In the meantime, having heard Bob's story on the news, a Wounded Warriors Project Alumna was so moved that she organized her chapter of Wounded Warriors to help on the renovation work. A local plumbing and heating company saw the story and donated and installed a brand-new HVAC system. Bob's generosity was inspiring others to give.

Bob had loved his neighborhood and his neighbors. He felt like that was part of what made the house something someone else might be able to enjoy. So when the dedication day arrived, it seemed appropriate that his neighbors were all there, as well as some of the volunteers, plus Mike, Lynda, Matt, and other Habitat staffers. But it also seemed appropriate that the crowd was small. Bob was not someone who wanted to be in the limelight, and the low-key nature of the ceremony felt right. The best part of the ceremony was that Bob was there.

The May day was bright and sunny. The grass was green. The house was immaculate with its new coat of paint and sparkling clean windows. Bonnie spoke to the small group. "Bob," she said, looking over at his still-handsome face, "you are the foundation. You cultivated this land. We cannot thank you enough."

Mike said, "Every gift we receive is special, but what Bob has done is tremendous. His generosity will live on for many years." Mike felt a lot of affection for this man who had given everything he had and was leaving with no fear, no bitterness, and only kindness, generosity, and love.

Bob had been able to drive himself from the assisted living facility to the ceremony. Now he sat instead of standing, with his oxygen tank beside him. He didn't speak at the ceremony—talking had become difficult—but Mike knew Bob probably wouldn't have wanted to say anything anyway or take any of the happy attention from Bonnie and her new home.

With Bonnie moved in and Bob resting comfortably in his apartment, life went on. Bonnie had kept a couch that originally belonged to Bob's mother. What did you need with a new couch when you had a perfectly good one? Especially one that had belonged to Bob. His pragmatic spirit was alive and well in the home where he'd spent so many years.

Lynda had one of Bob's chairs at her house. In a house

with seven children, not much was sacred when it came to furnishings, but that chair was another matter. "Don't jump on Bob's chair!" was a familiar plea in their happy, busy home, though Lynda had to admit seeing them climb all over it probably would have made Bob grin.

There was no obituary in the paper when Bob passed away. He was buried at Fort Snelling National Cemetery, his grave marker one among more than 175,000 identical white marble stones. Even in death, he draws no attention. Instead he lies in peace in this beautiful, quiet place with other veterans whose travels on earth are done.

ROBERT LEONARD KARLSTRAND
SSGT
US AIR FORCE
VIETNAM
DECEMBER 18, 1949
MAY 11, 2017
DEARLY LOVED

In Zambia I saw beautiful examples of generosity in action.

Learning from the Phiris

In 2010, I took my son, Alexander, a teenager at the time, to Zambia on his first overseas Habitat trip. The CEO of a Fortune 500 company and his family were part of the group as well, and I was the only one in the volunteer crew who'd ever been to Africa. I knew the volunteers' points of view would be changed forever by what they saw in Zambia, but as I'd come to learn from my own Habitat experiences around the world, it wasn't what you saw that you remembered and held in your heart but the people you met. And the people I met on this particular trip would forever become a touchstone for me when it comes to how to be truly generous. As Americans, I think, we make a pretty big show of our generosity at times. That can be completely appropriate, and it can inspire others to give as well, but in my daily life, I always want to be more like the Phiris.

Like a lot of other families in Zambia, where almost 65 percent of the people live on less than two dollars a day, the Phiris lived in what amounted to a tent, and barely a tent at that. The plastic tarps were torn and blew in the wind and let in the rain. The floor was dirt, and that dirt turned to mud during the rainy season. The tent started out as home to Mr. and Mrs. Phiri and their seven children.

Mr. Phiri and three of their children were suffering from tuberculosis. When Mr. Phiri's brother and sister-in-law died from AIDS, he and his wife took in four nieces and nephews. The tent was not large, but family was family. They wouldn't have considered turning their young nieces and nephews away. Then one of the Phiri sons met a teenager named Gift who was homeless. His mother had disappeared and his father had been abusive, so he had chosen to live on the streets doing odd jobs to make money. Maybe Gift wasn't technically family, but it was surprising how many people a makeshift tent could hold.

By the time we met the Phiri family, their modest tent was a loving home to fourteen people. At first glance, the community seemed like just an arbitrary location in an expanse of dirt. Nothing was paved, and there was red dust everywhere. There was no sanitation system. For Alexander, and probably for the other people seeing these living conditions for the first time, it was shocking to take it all in. And then it was hard not to feel a little bit guilty. Alexander thought about the silly things he and his friends at home complained about.

Gift was close to the age of Alexander and the other teenage boys with us, and the boys immediately hit it off. They were in charge of digging a hole for the ventilated pit latrine we would be installing. In the hard-packed dirt, this was no easy job. It was difficult to complain, though, because Gift never did. He only smiled.

Being a parent and looking at Gift and the Phiri kids, it was hard not to wonder how resilient my kids and their peers back home would be. Even in our roomy houses, if we had just one cousin stay with us for more than a week, sure, they'd be gracious—but for how long? And what if it was four cousins? And a guy we'd just met who didn't have a place to live? It was tough to imagine. Yet the Phiris were doing it with extremely limited resources and almost no space. While I marveled at their generosity, they went on about the business of showing love to their family members, original and new.

The Phiris' new house would hardly be a mansion, only four small rooms, but to them it was massive. To Alexander, even the new house seemed hardly to be a house, but to the Phiris, it would keep them dry when it rained and would provide shelter that was especially needed for the sick family members. As the days went on, I got to witness that magic transformation in Alexander's point of view: the Phiri children and Gift went from "these people on the other side of the world I'm helping out" to "just a group of kids."

Soccer proved a joyful common bond that helped this transformation along. Not only did the local kids know all the international soccer stars, but they were phenomenal players themselves. During a lunch-break soccer match, the local boys put on a clinic for the Americans. The pitch was a patch of dusty dirt. The goal posts were rocks. Most of the local kids went barefoot. The lucky ones had cheap flip-flops. The soccer ball was a bunch of plastic bags rolled into a big ball. And the local kids taught the Americans some moves and passes they had never seen.

I met another young woman in Zambia who exemplified the kind of resilience the Phiri kids showed. Her name was Dorcas Phiri (no relation to the other family), and she, too, had been living in a makeshift tent. Her father had died, and one day her mother simply disappeared. Dorcas was sixteen years old and was left to care for her younger siblings. For three years they lived in the crude jumble of materials that barely constituted a tent, grieving their father and wishing their mother would come home.

None of them were able to go to school. When it rained, they stood up for hours to avoid lying in mud. There was no way to keep out thieves. It would have been easy for Dorcas to leave her siblings to the care of someone else or even abandon them. She was a smart girl; she'd been good at school. She had the potential to get a career and follow her dreams. But as with the Phiris, there was nothing so bad in life that they couldn't help their family and loved ones through it together.

Dorcas continued to face all manner of unspeakable challenges and struggles just to keep her family alive and together. Somehow she never lost hope that things would get better. She never gave up on life.

When Habitat found her and her siblings, staffers immediately mobilized to help her. Simply to put one foot in front of the other, this young woman had undergone more strife than most would encounter in a lifetime. Through its program for orphans and vulnerable groups, Habitat was able to subsidize a new home for her and her siblings. Dorcas and her family only had to contribute sweat equity. The small home had a third room with its own entrance, so they could rent it out for extra income. Dorcas's siblings got to go back to school. She got a job and was eventually able to build more rooms onto their home for more rental income and to have electricity installed. Still, there was one past pain they never expected to be completely healed: the absence of their mother.

A few years later, however, Dorcas's mother did return, and they welcomed her with open arms. She said she had left their home that morning so long ago to go to Mozambique to buy fish she could bring back to Zambia to trade and sell. On her way, she had been robbed, and she had no money to get back and no way to contact Dorcas and her siblings. She now lives in the house that Dorcas and Habitat built, with two of the children and their grandmother. Dorcas and one sister are married and raising children of their own.

No one can know another person's pain, and no one can understand why some people are crushed by what from the outside looking in may appear to be minor setbacks in their lives and others are resilient in the face of the most harrowing catastrophes. What I do know is that I get immense inspiration from Dorcas and the Phiris. No pity. One foot in front of the other. One more day. A smile of hope. Happiness in the company of loved ones.

Selfishly, I felt like this trip would be an advantage for Alexander and the other American teenagers for the rest of their lives. They might not have been able to articulate it, but I knew there would be ripples that would show themselves as they navigated life ahead.

Randall Wallace, screenwriter of movies such as *Braveheart* and a devoted Habitat organizer and volunteer, captured the spirit of Habitat beautifully: "Habitat for Humanity is a perpetual motion miracle; everyone who receives, gives and everyone who gives, receives. If you want to live complacent and uninspired, stay away from Habitat. Come close to Habitat and it will change you and make you part of something that changes the world."

In the case of the Phiris, there was no doubt in my mind that as much as we were giving them something concrete to improve their lives, they were giving to us as well. They were thankful to see these people not just help them finance an affordable home but also come from so far away to physically help them build it. Their family was going from a barely habitable tent to proper shelter with a water system and sanitation. But you got the feeling that even if they had not been able to experience these improvements, they somehow would have found a way forward. I don't want to minimize the impact of a decent house for this family—their new situation was life-changing for them— but I also don't want to minimize the impact this family had on us, because it was life-changing for us, too.

You could go to these parts of Zambia as a tourist, but unless you got to be in a relationship with the people in a community, you wouldn't feel that personal connection with those who in some ways are so different from you and in some ways so similar. It's the difference between seeing a community and experiencing it, making the connection personal and relational.

That's a very real purpose of our Global Village program: relationships and education. These create respect and engagement that go beyond the time spent on the trips themselves. I have seen amazing transformations take place from changed hearts and new relationships that lead to lifelong personal connections and newfound humanitarian support for families all over the world. Where before these were abstract concepts, they become Gift, Dorcas, the children playing soccer. These connections create lifelong financial supporters and advocates for global affordable housing.

When volunteers are able to personally experience people on the other side of the world as their neighbors, they want to uplift them not out of a sense of charity but from a sense of doing the right thing for their fellow humans. The personal connections and transformations I've witnessed and get to experience are what make me feel like part of the world and part of the larger dynamic universe of God's creation.

The way the neighborhood children crowded around us to welcome us, play with us, and talk to us, the way the women from the community fixed us lunch each day, and the way the Phiris opened up their hearts and hospitality to us when we thought we were supposed to be the ones helping them exemplified that perpetual motion miracle when the givers and the receivers get all mixed up and everybody walks away with more than they came with.

The Phiris taught me by example how to make room even when I think I don't have it. They taught me to share when I think I can't. To give whatever I have and know that I'll be OK.

In America, we make a big deal when we give. We throw parties, name things after each other, and give awards to showcase our contributions. There's nothing wrong with that, because being able to give is certainly worth celebrating, and inspiring others to do the same is even better. It can start a movement of giving. But what I think of when I think of the Phiris is the kind of life-changing giving that's not celebrated and not even mentioned. It's just done because it's the right thing to do.

7

Service

THE ACTUAL ACT of doing something, of being useful, as my grandmother always used to remind me, amplifies all of the other virtues in this book. My grandmother Millicent Fenwick and my godmother, Jill Ker Conway, were two very important role models for me when it came to having a purpose in life and serving others.

I believe that for both of them a large part of their motivation to serve was a response to hardship and sadness. Both of them could so easily have shrunk away from life because of early setbacks, but instead they turned outward and soared.

Jill was my closest mentor and guide until her passing in 2018. Her complete CV would take up several pages in this book, but here are some of the highlights.

By the age of seven, Jill was doing the same strenuous labor as her two big brothers on the family sheep farm in the extremely isolated wilds of the Australian outback. Her only education was homeschooling from her mother one day a week, but this took a backseat to tending the 32,000-acre ranch. With the onset of a deadly drought, everything fell apart for the family.

When she was ten, her father drowned while trying to fix a water pipe. Her mother tried to keep the farm going, but the drought persisted, and the family was deeply in debt. They moved to Sydney, where she and her brothers experienced profound culture shock. She went to boarding school and finally found the academic environment her eager mind had been craving. After graduating with honors from the University of Sydney and winning the University Medal in History, she applied for a position in the Australian foreign service. She was turned down by the all-male selection committee, while her male classmates were accepted. This was a heartbreak that went on to fuel a lifetime of fighting for women's equality.

Jill earned her PhD from Harvard, where she met the love of her life, John Conway, a Canadian professor of history who had been a mentor to my father. Jill and John married in 1962, the year I was born. Jill began her career as a history professor and then became vice president at the University of Toronto. She became an administrator because when she discovered deep pay inequities for women professors and protested, they put her in charge of fixing it. Jill was the first woman to be president of Smith College, where she doubled their endowment. She advocated for students on financial aid and students who'd had to take time off or cut back their studies because of work and family obligations. She wrote several books, including her bestselling memoir *The Road from Coorain*.

After her retirement she served on the board of a nonprofit focusing on homelessness, particularly among veterans. John was a World War II hero who'd jumped on a grenade to save his company, losing an arm in the process, so veterans' issues was another cause that was dear to her. In 2013, President Barack Obama presented her with a National Humanities Medal.

Jill had the remarkable gift of presence. I'll never forget a night when I went to visit her at Smith when I was in junior high. We had a long, wonderful dinner, and even though I was only thirteen years old and she probably had hours of work waiting for her on her desk, she made me feel like I was the center of the world and what I had to say was important. Whenever I had a big life decision, I would always make a pilgrimage to see her and get her advice.

Service was everything to Jill. Despite the losses and disappointments she'd been through, she chose to focus on the blessings. She lived a long, full life, but I still mourn her passing.

Another one of my role models and a person I would never want to disappoint was my grandmother. Grandma had a larger-than-life personality and, like Jill, went through her share of tragedy. When she was five years old, her mother and father were on the *Lusitania* when it was sunk by a German U-boat. Tragically, her mother died when her lifeboat overturned. He survived by clinging to wreckage, but he went on to marry a difficult woman with whom Grandma never had a good relationship. Her father was a passive presence, deferring to his wife's wishes.

Grandma was a brilliant person who spoke multiple languages fluently, but she never graduated from high school. She scandalously married a charming divorcé who turned out to be as unreliable as everyone had warned her he was. He decamped for Europe in 1938, leaving her with two young children and his debts, which she was determined to pay off. Without a high school diploma, however, she had a hard time finding a job. She finally got hired as a writer for *Vogue* and in 1948 wrote *Vogue's Book of Etiquette,* which sold a million copies. But it was in her later years that she finally got to live out her ferocious drive for social justice.

She started on the local level, serving on the school board and lobbying for a public swimming pool for her community. She then served in the New Jersey legislature and on the New Jersey Commission on Civil Rights. She earned the nickname "Outhouse Millie" for her efforts to improve sanitation facilities for migrant farm workers. She led the Department of Consumer Affairs for New Jersey and then, at the age of sixty-four, in 1974, was elected to the US Congress. A striking figure at five foot eleven, she wore the same Italian suits she'd been wearing for more than three decades and her signature pearls. Her doctor had told her she had to stop smoking cigarettes, so she got around that by smoking a pipe.

Wayne Hays, the powerful chair of the Ways and Means Committee, once said he was going to withhold pay from her staff "if that woman doesn't sit down and keep quiet." She was polite. Her manners were impeccable. But she never backed down.

Her proudest legislative work was an enforcement mechanism for the Helsinki Accords, the first global human rights framework. Walter Cronkite called her the "conscience of Congress," and it was said she was the model for Garry Trudeau's *Doonesbury* character Lacey Davenport. She was absolutely tireless. She responded to constituent letters with handwritten letters of her own. She mailed personal checks to the US Treasury after Congress approved a raise for itself that she disagreed with. After her years in office, Ronald Reagan appointed her US representative to the United Nations Food and Agriculture Organization, based in Rome. Where life had sometimes taken from her, she filled it with service and a determination for justice.

The first time I introduced her to the woman who became my wife, Ashley and I were just friends. Grandma was very impressed with Ashley, who had just graduated from law school, and they immediately hit it off. Much later, when we went to see her again and I told her that Ashley and I were engaged, without taking a breath, she took the beloved ring her best friend had given her decades before off her finger, the only ring she wore, and gave it to Ashley as an engagement ring. That was very touching to me because I knew that friendship meant a great deal to her and that she was not one to take relationships lightly.

In fact, we got into a conversation that day about love and justice. Yes, the three of us agreed, you needed both. But which was more important? Love or justice? Ashley was making a theological case for love, and my grandmother—which was so rare for her—said, "You know, you're right." She didn't stop there, though. She went on, "But we've got to have justice because you can't always count on love."

Grandma was right, too, of course, but it made me sad because I knew she had been disappointed by those she'd counted on to love her—her father, her stepmother, her husband—and had been devastated by the loss of her mother and the premature death of her sister, who was her closest friend. She had dedicated her life to justice, perhaps partly as an outlet for her personal grief. She knew from her own life that humans were frail and love was not a sure thing, so there'd better be a legal framework in place operating outside of human emotions. I had great admiration and a little awe for how determined she was to improve conditions for others.

I think about how the theologian Frederick Buechner describes vocation: "The place God calls you to is the place where your deep gladness and the world's deep hunger meet." In other words, your calling is a combination of what you want to do and what the world needs.

I'm a little skeptical when we tell everyone, "Go find your passion!" To me, it's deeper. It's really about purpose. Passion is a piece of it, but it's got to be passion plus ability plus a mission that matters. When I think of Grandma and Jill, they exemplify this combination. They didn't take their calling or their service lightly. In fact, they believed it was part of their spiritual responsibility.

Your calling may not be the same as your job. Whether it is or isn't, if you can, do some volunteer work. Service doesn't have to take up a lifetime to become life-changing. Do whatever you can do to be useful, and I'm willing to bet you'll want to do more.

Service has played a part in all of the stories in this book, but in this chapter in particular I think you'll see how joyful it can be, and how cathartic and humbling. Above all, service is a way to connect with our fellow human beings. When we connect on the common ground we share doing something useful, we experience true community.

On a practical level, it's also a great way to forget about yourself for a little while and make new friends. I've joked for many years that I want to start a Habitat dating service because I know so many couples who met on a Habitat build site. It's a great place to meet somebody with a similar worldview and a desire to serve. And that's a great thing to want in a partner, right?

By serving others, we become our best selves, our better angels.

———

There's adventure in service. Even if you volunteer with an organization in your hometown, you can meet people you've never met before who can expose you to whole new worlds of experience. If you go global, the potential is even more expansive. It's not so much where you go and what you see but who you meet and what you learn.

Adventures in Honeymooning

Forget room service. Forget rose petals sprinkled over a fantasy suite. Forget dinner and dancing in a nightclub. And don't even think about a spa treatment. No, instead put on your work gloves and mix some mortar. Lisa Ofstedal and Andy Wahlstrom, *this* is your honeymoon adventure.

Lisa and Andy were well settled into their careers when they got engaged. They both had plenty of sheets, pots, pans, and dishes. They didn't need any wedding presents—they were simply happy to celebrate with family and friends. For those who wanted to give a gift anyway, they asked for donations toward a Habitat Global Village build in Udon Thani, Thailand, where they were going to volunteer. For this couple from Minnesota, the warm climate of Thailand would be a luxury in and of itself. They weren't there to be pampered, though. In their mind, what better way to build a solid foundation for their life together than to literally start building?

So they jumped right in. Every morning, they'd hit the breakfast buffet at the hotel—no breakfast in bed when there's adventure waiting—and fuel up for the day on the site. The forty-five-minute bus ride was a nice way to prepare for the build. They got to chat with the other volunteers and get to know them.

Once on the site, their site leader, Bank, was there to greet them. He was a fun-loving, friendly, energetic guy. He was passionate about aerobics, and he wasn't the only one. It was a hugely popular pastime to wait for nightfall when the temperatures were cooler and then convene in a Tesco Lotus grocery store parking lot with about a hundred other people and do a mass aerobics session. Bank was one of the leaders. So first thing every morning on the worksite, Bank would crank up some tunes and lead the volunteers in an aerobics routine. Lisa and Andy laughed their way through it, and sure enough, it did loosen up the muscles and any nerves or shyness among the group. The volunteers were warmed up and ready to go. Lisa and Andy would get their tasks for the day, at first simply grunt work like forming a human assembly line passing buckets and then settling in to build a brick wall together.

Lisa and Andy were meticulous about their wall. This was going to be someone's home, and they wanted it to be right. They knew they would want it done with love and attention if it were their home, and that was how they approached it now as they carefully stacked one brick and then another, checking with the site supervisors to make sure they were doing it correctly and straight enough. At

first communication with the Thai workers and homeowners was a little challenging, but by the end of the week, the
thumbs-up and other gestures had become second nature.
It was satisfying to see their wall getting taller every day,
and managing to stay straight in the process. For a seemingly simple task, it wasn't easy to do well, and they were
proud of their progress.

Both of them had very busy work schedules at home, so
it was rare for them to spend this much time literally side
by side. Luckily, they found they didn't get sick of each
other. In fact, having each other there made the experience
of this place and these people more real, and they knew
they would always remember their honeymoon as something much more than just a vacation together.

This was Lisa's first global building trip, but she was
no stranger to traveling while volunteering. She had taught
English in the central mountains of Costa Rica, where
she lived with a host family on their blackberry and coffee
farm. She and Andy had gone back and stayed with the
family on a visit. That was what she and Andy loved about
their experiences traveling and helping people—the relationships that developed. Often the people you connected
with became lifelong friends. At the very least you could
keep up with them on social media. Even if you never got
to see or hear from a person again, you'd shared something
special and learned from each other. The way each person
you'd connected with had made an impression on you,

the way they made you think or feel—that was way better than any souvenir you could take back home.

Andy had been doing Habitat service trips since college. Being from Minnesota, he didn't know any other students when he transferred to the University of North Carolina, so his first year there he did a Habitat trip during one of the school breaks and found out it was a great way to meet people and do something worthwhile at the same time. He went on more Habitat trips to Miami, Ethiopia, and Texas. Even on the domestic trips, he appreciated the cultural exchanges and connections. On the trip to Texas, he took with him his friend Omar, a Somali immigrant by way of London. That was a cultural exchange in itself.

On this trip, he was enjoying spending time with Lisa and making friends with the other volunteers and the Thai people together as a couple. For them to be immersed as newlyweds in an unfamiliar community, instead of being paying guests at a fancy resort, made their honeymoon an adventure. Being embraced by that community as they worked on their wall made it that much more rewarding.

One afternoon on the worksite, Bank suggested they all knock off a little early. Some of the volunteers didn't want to miss a minute of working, but Bank assured them it was OK. There was a parade for a new temple that was being built, and he wanted them all to see it.

Hundreds of people were dancing in the parade. A group of women invited Lisa and some of the other women from Habitat to join them and showed them how to do the steps as they progressed down the street. Lisa joined right in, doing the steps the best she could as they danced toward the temple. Behind them at the end of the parade was a truck with a wall of speakers blasting music—not nearly as sturdy a wall as Lisa and Andy's. There were so many speakers piled on top of each other, almost falling over the side of the truck, that it seemed like it could collapse at any minute.

Around the temple were booths, and for a few baht— one baht was worth about three American cents—you could draw a ticket. Each ticket had a number on it that correlated to a prize. The people in the booth would take your ticket and disappear behind the booth and come back with the prize. Andy won an orange drink. Another American in the Habitat group won an eight-foot-tall broom.

On another excursion with the volunteer crew, Lisa and Andy went to Sala Keoku, a sculpture garden in the forest. The massive scale of the statues astonished them. They gasped out loud when they rounded some trees and there, towering sixty-five feet above them, was a seven-headed snake, one of the mythical creatures called Naga. Its fangs were sharp, and its forked tongues were about ten feet long. Its hooded heads formed a protective canopy over a meditating Buddha.

Near the end of the week, some of the locals gave Lisa a bouquet made from native flowers. In her work pants and T-shirt instead of a white dress, she threw the bouquet to the group. When it was time to go, Lisa and Andy's wall was in good form, part of a family's new home that would shelter them and keep them safe. It was an emotional good-bye as the homeowners thanked everyone and embraced them.

This honeymoon adventure had been more than just a fun trip, and more than a working trip. It was a meaningful start to an even longer journey for the couple. Together, they were able to test themselves in a place where they didn't know the language or culture. Instead of coming from a place of confidence and knowing it all, they both had to start from a humble place of not knowing all that much. Realizing the value of humility over hubris and being able to humble oneself could go a long way in a marriage.

Lisa and Andy now have a young daughter. They're focused on building a home of love and stability for her. But it won't be long before they'll be taking her with them on a whole new set of family adventures. It's never too early to learn that giving is receiving.

Yes, some of my role models are teenagers.

Legacy

For sixteen straight Saturdays, high school junior Taylor Thompson worked on the Habitat build site where homeowner Annette Lopez and her four-year-old daughter Isabella would start their new life. It was a new life for Taylor, too. Instead of soccer, a mainstay of his Saturday mornings for as long as he could remember, there was no place he would rather be than here at 7:30 a.m., cutting lumber, hammering nails, placing shingles, hanging cabinets, caulking baseboards. Whatever was needed, his hands were eager to do it. The movement of his body, the exertion of his muscles, the sounds of saws and drills were what his mind and heart craved throughout the week. He couldn't wait to get to the site. To do something.

When the crew of "regulars" finished at about 4:30 in the afternoon, they'd go into a home that had already been framed to hang out for an hour. They'd been volunteering together a long time, but the regulars took Taylor into the fold, no questions asked. They knew why Taylor was working so hard on this house, and they respected that. Plus the kid had energy, and they could always use that on the site. As Taylor himself became a regular, they'd give him bottles of Topo Chico sparkling water while they enjoyed their bottles of beer at the end of a long day. They'd talk about nothing in particular—sports, their families, what was going on in their lives.

It had been over a year since Taylor's mother, Maureen Thompson, had passed away from breast cancer, a year of starting every day without her. Here on the worksite, he couldn't help but feel her presence. He wasn't able to hug her or talk to her out loud, but he could build something. He could do something she would be proud of.

Taylor's father, Gary, made sure the family didn't wallow in their grief, didn't fall down and stay down. Instead of dwelling on what they were missing, Gary, Taylor, and his two younger sisters, Kyla and Katelyn, focused on what they would always have of Maureen—all the passions she possessed: her love for them, her work as an architect, her creativity, her deep friendships, and her desire to help other people. When Taylor felt his grief creeping in, he would think about what his mother would want him to do. "Do something!" he could almost hear her say. "Change the world!"

For Taylor, all of his mother's passions and hopes for him came together on the build site. It had started with his need to complete a service project on his road to becoming an Eagle Scout. He had been brainstorming ideas for the project with his dad while they were on a long car drive. That was when he thought of the perfect way to make a lasting impact on a community: sponsoring and building a Habitat for Humanity home.

It took months to complete the paperwork and begin the necessary conversations with Austin Habitat for Humanity to make this dream a reality. When he presented the idea to the local council of the Boy Scouts of America, however, they said they had not been anticipating something this "ambitious." At the time, Taylor had no idea what a blessing this pushback would prove to be. Now he realized this project was not just about completing a requirement. Not about an Eagle Scout project.

Not about an award. It was about love. A son's love for his mom.

When Maureen was a master's student at the University of Texas at Austin's School of Architecture, she had competed in a design competition where the winner got the opportunity to build a Habitat for Humanity home using their own design. The home wouldn't have air conditioning, so the architecture students had to be creative with the shape of the house to enable maximum airflow and allow for cross-ventilation. The U-shaped design Maureen's team created won the competition, and they were able to help build the home. She was so passionate about it that her parents came to Austin from South Carolina to help with construction themselves. Inspired by their daughter's work, they decided they, too, should get involved with Habitat. That determination led them to work on more than seventy homes over the years, serve on their local affiliate's board, and travel on multiple Global Village build trips.

Taylor took up the mantle in memory of his mom and in honor of her legacy. He would become the third generation of Habitat builders in the family.

To sponsor a home, he'd have to raise $85,000. He wasn't daunted. Like his parents, like his grandparents, he believed a passion was something worth pursuing no matter how much effort or sacrifice it would require. As his dad often told him, "It takes the same amount of time to do something big as it does to do something small. So why not just do something big?" Instead of abandoning his idea when the Scouts doubted him, he doubled down on it. He knew he would have to forge his own path. If he wanted to follow this passion, he would have to go after it, his own way.

With his father's help, he began to solicit donations, slowly at first, including a contribution from O'Connell Robertson, the architecture firm where Maureen had pursued her professional passion and where she'd worked until the week before she passed. He had been nervous about talking to people and asking them to donate, but he soon got over it. Leaving his fears behind, with his mind and heart set on his goal instead, he raised the money in only three months.

He began the actual construction with the Habitat crew of volunteers feeling as if his mother was looking on, proud of him for channeling his grief into doing something to help someone and proud of him for figuring things out and making his vision become a reality. And with hard work, a reality it became: The house was soon finished (and Taylor *did* make Eagle Scout).

If Taylor ever feels a little overwhelmed or a little unsure in life, he grounds himself by remembering the dedication ceremony for Annette's home. During the days leading up to the ceremony, he had pictured how it all would go. He'd never factored in the possibility he might cry. Despite all his family had been through, he wasn't an emotional person, especially on the outside. And yet as he gave Annette the key, her face beaming with pride and appreciation, he

was caught by surprise at the stinging heaviness building behind his eyes. He hugged Annette and then quietly
made his way to the back of the crowd for the rest of the
ceremony. One tear escaped and rolled hotly down his
cheek. Then another. And another. And they kept coming.

As the crowd in front of him clapped and cheered, their
attention on Annette, the tears overcame him in a wave
of emotion that had been building for the last two years.
Tears of love for his mom. Tears for the love his mother had
for him. Tears for his dad and sisters and how strong they
had been. Tears of love for Annette and Isabella and their
new home. Tears of love for what he was doing—showing
up early Saturday mornings and doing something for
somebody. Tears of exhaustion. Tears of relief. Tears that
it was over. Tears of fear for the uncertainty of what came
next. Tears of fear that he might not ever feel as close to his
mother as he had working on the site.

But it didn't have to be over. He could do it again
and again. If he could help people while doing what he
loved, then he was definitely following in his mother's
footsteps.

His mother's legacy was still alive in all the homes she
created, including that very first Habitat home, which Taylor
was surprised to find out was located only two blocks from
Annette's. One day while working on Annette's house,
Taylor and his dad walked over to see it. The same homeowner from twenty years before was still living there. Her
daughter had gone to college and started a family of her

own. Her grandson now played in the rooms Taylor's mom had designed and helped build with her own hands.

Maureen's legacy is also still alive in her three children and whatever passions they choose to pursue. Taylor feels lucky to have found his passion for Habitat so early and to be able to do what he loves while changing other people's lives. Since helping build Annette's house, he has worked on three Carter Work Projects and on a Global Village build in Thailand, and participated in two Habitat on the Hill legislative conferences in Washington, DC.

Taylor is a third-year student at the University of Virginia. He plans to finish his undergraduate degree in design-thinking architecture before beginning a master's in public policy while continuing to help lead the university's Habitat for Humanity campus chapter. Following the completion of his degrees, he'd like to buy a one-way ticket to the other end of the world and spend a year building with different Habitat affiliates around the globe.

I got to build with Taylor on two Carter Work Projects. It's great to see how service has worked magic in Taylor's life and how he has worked magic through service. He was able to respond to his grief and at the same time connect with the memory of his mother and help his whole family heal.

In the process, he was able to find his passion in life and forge a path to pursue it. When we feel helpless in the face of what is going on in our personal lives, or even what's going on in the world, just doing something, physically serving, can lead to healing and connection. If you're in doubt, try it.

This is a story Habitat volunteers love to tell.
Bill Metzger witnessed it firsthand and can testify
that some legends are absolutely the real deal.

Humble Hero

Bill Metzger and his son, Stein, were volunteer house leaders for a five-day Habitat build in the Philippines in 1999. It was the last afternoon of the build.

They'd been told to complete as much as they could on their houses, and then a local crew of professionals would take over whatever the volunteer crews were unable to finish. The volunteers had worked insanely hard that last day to get as much done as possible. The house Bill was in charge of was about 95 percent finished.

After five long days of work, his crew was exhausted. Standing outside the house, feeling pretty good about how much work they had completed, Bill was pleased and surprised to see President Carter walking down the road.

Everyone who'd been working on the houses called out to him as he passed, "Mr. President! Mr. President!"

They all wanted to have their picture taken with him. He was kind and gentle and said, "No, thank you." He was intent on checking the progress of the houses. He and Mrs. Carter had finished their own house, but he cared deeply about the project as a whole and how each leader would be leaving his or her home.

As he walked toward Bill, Bill was thinking, *What am I going to say to the president?*

Before he had a chance to say anything, President Carter asked, "You got your toilet in?"

Well, that wasn't the question Bill had been expecting. "No, sir," he said.

"Can I show you how to do it?"

"Yes, sir." As if he'd say no to the president!

"Come with me."

In the bathroom there was a drain hole, and in the corner sat the toilet and a bag of mortar.

President Carter said, "Mix up some of that mortar over there."

So Bill mixed it up.

"Now you watch," President Carter said.

The president got down on his hands and knees. He spread the mortar around the drainage hole. Then he gently set the toilet into the mortar. He pulled out his level from his tool belt and leveled the toilet both ways to make sure it was on there just right.

Seventy-five years old, and there he was on his hands and knees, setting that toilet.

"OK," the president said. "Can you show your son how to do that?"

Bill said, "Yes, sir," and off the president went.

There was no chitchat. No shaking of hands or patting of backs. He was on the job. He didn't want to leave until every home had a working toilet.

So Bill went over to Stein's house next door, and he passed on what the president had taught him.

As I write this, I'm looking forward to October, when only a few days after his ninety-fifth birthday, this gentle, caring, no-nonsense volunteer will be working on a Habitat build site again for a full week, as he has since 1984, this time in Nashville, Tennessee.

Acknowledgments

I am grateful for so many people who helped bring this book to life. This book wouldn't have been possible without my Habitat family. In keeping with the spirit of this book, 100 percent of my proceeds from the sale of the book are going directly to Habitat to further our mission.

First, President and Mrs. Carter—Thank you for your inspiration, modeling faith in action, and putting Habitat on the map. In 1984, when you got on a bus from Plains to spend a week rehabbing a tenement building in New York and sleeping in a church basement, you forever changed Habitat and the post-presidency. It has been one of the great privileges of my life to work alongside you the past fourteen years.

Bessie Gantt, my collaborator, for all the time, care, and attention in helping research and infuse our stories with such joy and heart.

To Chris Clarke and Shala Carlson for shaping and

advancing the ways in which we tell the global Habitat story and to Pam Campbell, Ann Hardie, and our communications team for all the groundwork and shepherding of the project.

My colleagues at Habitat. It is a joy and blessing to do this work alongside you.

My old friend Will Schwalbe and his team at St. Martin's Essentials, for envisioning the book and believing in it. Thank you to Andrea Mosqueda. To the marketing and publicity team, especially Brant Janeway, Marissa Sangiacomo, and Rebecca Lang. And to publishing director Anne-Marie Tallberg and editorial director Joel Fotinos for all their support. I'm so thankful for the book to be in such good hands.

Amy Hughes for helping us navigate the publishing world—for your wisdom and guidance.

To all the Habitat homebuyers and their families who represent the millions of families with whom we've partnered around the world. Thank you for your resilience, generosity, and leadership. You exemplify the virtues in this book and are why we build: Dorothy Howard, Geta Heradea, Angel Meza, Granny from Lesotho, Crystal Hardy, Jose Tobar, Antonia Cuffee and her mother, Valerie, Eric Garcia, Chan Ksor and Y'Thao Nai, Unziyamoh Abulhaeva, Shalini and Subhash Sathe, Sadhiya and Aziz Sheikh, Subeyda Asmaeel and Haroun Osman, Anita Stewart, the Phiri Family, Dorcas Phiri, and Boris Henderson.

Thank you, Denise Gavala, whose parents' home was part of the Habitat veterans program.

To the volunteers and Habitat staff who shared their stories. Thank you for living these virtues every day: Bill Murphy, Deirdre Glenn, Donna Ricca, Alan Brown, Allison Brammer, Paul Levitt, Vic Romback, Jim Lempke, Dang Phan, Hope Hartman, Alexander Reckford, Lisa Ofstedal and Andy Wahlstrom, Taylor Thompson, and Bill Metzger. Corey Allen from Habitat for Humanity of Greater Newburgh, Jenny Williams from Habitat Northern Ireland, Blake Strayhorn from Habitat for Humanity of Durham, and from Twin Cities Habitat for Humanity, Mike Nelson, Matt Haugen, and Lynda Bouley.

To leaders from our affiliates and community who gave a helping hand: Angela Cox and Allison Hay from Houston Habitat for Humanity, Diana Giuliano from Northern Ocean Habitat for Humanity, Robyn Burns of Habitat for Humanity of Metro Denver, Matt Arbolino from Habitat for Humanity of Greater Newburgh, JoAnn Hansen from Habitat for Humanity Choptank, Andrea McKenna from Habitat for Humanity of Collier County, Phil Prince from Habitat for Humanity of Charlotte, Rich Cooke and Blair Bravo from Morris Habitat for Humanity, Chris Untiet from Habitat for Humanity of Greater Los Angeles, Roxanne Little from Habitat for Humanity of Durham, and Brian Juntti from Twin Cities Habitat for Humanity. Thanks to John Warwick, Stein Metzger, and Jill Claflin.

To the millions of families, staff, donors, and volunteers of the broader Habitat family who make our work possible. God never said it would be easy, just that it would be good. It isn't easy, but you make it good!

And especially to my wife, Ashley, and my children, Alexander, Grace, and Lily, for your love, patience, and support of me in this great adventure. I love you always.

Resource Guide

How to Get Involved

Families around the world partner with Habitat for Humanity to build or improve a place they can call home. We welcome all to join us in our mission of bringing people together to build homes, communities, and hope.

Habitat for Humanity's vision is a world where everyone has a decent place to live. Habitat homeowners help build their own homes alongside volunteers and pay an affordable mortgage or loan. We currently work in more than 70 countries and have helped more than 22 million people with improved living conditions since 1976.

Habitat for Humanity operates at the local level. Each Habitat for Humanity organization coordinates its own construction and selects local homebuyer applicants. Many operate local ReStore home improvement centers.

Opportunities to lend your support to Habitat exist in more than 1,000 communities throughout the United States. In the U.S., Habitat works in all fifty states, the District of Columbia, and Puerto Rico. In Canada, we build in all ten provinces and in each of the three territories. At www.habitat.org/where-we-build you can browse our country profiles and learn more about our work to build strength, stability, and independence with families throughout the world.

A few hours of your time doing simple construction tasks can help with building new homes or making needed repairs to homes of older homeowners, veterans, and families with too few resources. No prior construction experience or skills are necessary. Groups from corporations, faith organizations, and clubs can make a big difference on a construction site and experience teamwork and fellowship in the process. Many volunteers find joy and satisfaction building with families in distant countries and cultures far different from their own, creating connections with and learning from their global neighbors.

Some volunteers choose to give their time through Habitat ReStores or donate items to their local ReStore, which helps fund Habitat's work and keep useful items out of local landfills. Future Habitat homeowners participate in classroom work to help them learn to more effectively manage their homes and resources. Many volunteers choose to lend their time to supporting these programs. Long-term opportunities exist through the Habitat for Humanity Ameri-

Corps program. An exciting and growing area of our work is advocating with policymakers at all levels of government to make housing more affordable for families with modest incomes. Learn more about all the ways we work at www.habitat.org/impact/our-work.

We welcome all people to our work and encourage everyone to find the place in our organization that feels best to them. We invite you to be a part of the change you'd like to see in your community and the world. For those who don't have time to volunteer but would still like to help, Habitat welcomes your financial support.